PRINCIPLES
TO FORTUNE

Crafting a Culture to Massively Grow a Business

Scott J. Bintz

PRAISE FOR PRINCIPLES TO FORTUNE

"I was impressed with Scott Bintz's commitment to culture from the first time I met him some years ago. He was able to grow a business from a hobby business to a multi-million dollar e-commerce enterprise. His book, *Principles to Fortune*, demonstrates what the true mojo is in companies—the people. RealTruck's commitment to make people's lives better was the secret sauce to their profound and unprecedented success. If you want to increase brand loyalty from your employees, your customers and even your strategic business partnerships, then you need to read *Principles to Fortune*. The book is based upon the principles Scott used within his own company, with concrete examples that can be adopted and adapted to most any company culture."
—*Chip Conley, NYT Bestselling author, Hospitality Disruptor, Strategic Change Agent*

"Packed with business values you would expect from North Dakota. Scott Bintz's new book, *Principles to Fortune*, is an inspiring and wonderful read for those who run a business and those who want to start a new business."
—*Byron Dorgan, Former U.S. Senator*

"Fun, exciting and a joy to read. Full of business growth, marketing and culture insights wrapped up with emotional connections that truly inspire. *Principles to Fortune* provides superb examples of how to get employee engagement right through value led business practices. This book will energize anyone who has ever dreamed big."
—*Beth McConahay, Director of Marketing, UPS*

"Packed with real experience and wisdom for growing a business. Bintz's book, *Principles to Fortune*, shows how getting your company culture right, has game-changing results. Read it now!"
—*Garrett Moon, CEO & Co-Founder of CoSchedule, Author of 10X Marketing Formula*

"I've worked with many different types of companies and search engine optimization (SEO) is much easier and gets better results when you are working with a company that has a desire to improve and a willingness to take risks to get it done it. The book, *Principles to Fortune* shares how company culture can really impact a companies success in today's competitive marketplace."
—*Ken Colborn, SEO & Analytics at Avalara*

"Scott Bintz gives another example of how company culture can have a positive impact on people."
—*Tony Hsieh, CEO of Zappos*

"I had the fortune of watching Scott Bintz grow his e-commerce company from a fledgling hole in the wall to a company that competed amongst the giants. Scott's unique approach to growing his company came to garner the respect of the largest players in the industry. What was fascinating is how Scott did it his way, on his terms, all the while embracing a unique brand of culture as the centerpiece of his company. I always admired Scott's out of the box approach, which seemed to set aside the stiffness of corporate culture and rely more on what he knew to be real. The fact that he has taken the time to carefully and insightfully outline his journey, lessons and wisdom in his book *Principles to Fortune*, is a blessing to us all. A great read from front to back."
—*Julian Maimin, CEO of Reacha & Co-Founder of BAK Industries*

"*Principles to Fortune* is written for anyone in business. It's entertaining, full of surprises and insights. Scott Bintz shares the experience of creating a winning business culture with almost unbelievable results, right from the tiny state of North Dakota. Marketing, e-commerce and work culture all packed into a wonderful and inspiring read."
—*James Key Lim, CEO of FutureProof Marketing*

"Scott Bintz has long been a pioneer in e-commerce but is most recognized for creating a culture the led to his company's meteoric rise. The concepts in this book, *Principles to Fortune* lay out those principles and provide an outline which has had a lasting impact on my own business."
—*Bob Wolf, President of ICI*

"*Principles to Fortune* is a guide for those seeking success in the e-commerce field. It is also a remarkable defense for the central importance of culture in a business organization. Scott Bintz understands how to be successful in both arenas as a result of growing a truck accessory start-up into an Internet Retailers 14th 'Fastest Growing in the Top 500.' I especially appreciate Scott's willingness to share his knowledge with students, other entrepreneurs, and community leaders. This book is a natural extension of his instinctive gift for teaching."
—*Robert Badal, President of University of Jamestown 2002-2018*

"A great formula for business success. Scott Bintz's book, *Principles to Fortune* is written for leaders who want to up the game. Packed with insights for really taking care of employees, customers and business partners."
—*Carol Rogne, CEO of DFC Consultants, Ltd.*

"This isn't just another 'How to Make Millions Selling Online' book focusing on achievement and profit. It's much deeper and meaningful. It's Scott's authentic story of integrating core principles into his business to build a strong culture and help he and his team find personal purpose while doing so. The people at RealTruck happened to be building an eCommerce business but the strategies outlined in this book can be applied to any business. If fast money and power are your top priorities, don't read this book. If creating true fortune in life through business is, read it and adopt this as one of your guide books."
—*Clint Howitz, Founder & CEO of dogIDs.com*

"I love this story. Leading by principle takes guts, smarts and unwavering dedication. Not only is it the right way to build, lead and grow a business, it is the only way. Scott's principle-led proof and advice culminate in this real world story about RealTruck.com. Now, we can all benefit from and be inspired by this outrageously successful, against-all-odds story of an American-born entrepreneur."
—*Sandra Zoratti, Co-Founder & Chief Marketing Officer at The Marketing Network*

"If you want to take your business to the next level, *Principles to Fortune* by Scott Bintz, is a must read. It is full of valuable tools and principles to help you excel in your business. Winning on the race track or in business doesn't come easy, or by a ccident. Check out his story how he came from the bottom, all the way to the top!"
—*Dustin Strand, 2-Time Wissota National Champion Driver*

"In *Principles to Fortune*, the insights shared by Scott Bintz are enlightening. As a hard working North Dakota Entrepreneur, Scott leveraged culture to build RealTruck into a $100 million business. This is a must-read if you wish to accelerate your personal and business growth."
—*Marlo Anderson, Founder of National Day Calendar*

"Principles become action only through experience, by seeing them work on a daily basis. When those principles are focused on for an entire book by someone you know, an AHA moment is created for the reader. Scott Bintz has done just that. His blend of what is best for the customer and the employee reinforce much of what is necessary for success. Scott uses his personal success with RealTruck to develop a process focused on learning and asking the question, 'How do I make today better for our customers and our employees?' "
—*Bill Kennedy, Author & Development Director JRVLS*

"Scott is the real deal. He has built companies to massive scale, created engaging cultures, and made a tremendous impact in his community. Now, he breaks down his ideas into simple steps that each of us can apply. The best part about the book is that its not all about business, its about personal growth too."
—*Greg Tehven, Emerging Prairie Co-Founder*

First published by Red Headed Rebel®
1618 Hwy 281 N
Jamestown, ND 58401
www.RedHeadedRebel.com

Soft Cover: ISBN-13: 978-0-9996234-0-4 ISBN-10: 0-9996234-0-0
Hard Cover: ISBN-13: 978-0-9996234-1-1 ISBN-10: 0-9996234-1-9
E-Book: ISBN-13: 978-0-9996234-2-8 ISBN-10: 0-9996234-2-7
Library of Congress Control Number: 2018942140

To my mother, for her never-ending love and support. For always being my #1 fan.

To my bride, for her patience and love.

To our children, for your love and individual spirits.

To the people who helped build RealTruck: thank you.

CONTENTS

FOREWORD   IX

PREFACE   XIII

Why Read This Book?   *xiv*

1 THE BIG DEAL   **1**

The Million-Dollar Call   *1*
How The Hell Did You Get There?   *8*

2 AGAINST THE WIND   **11**

RealTruck Begins   *13*
The Brutal Facts   *15*
Changing The Market   *18*
Full-Time RealTruck   *21*
The Racetrack   *30*

3 CREATING CULTURE   **35**

How To Fail At Creating Culture   *39*
RealTruck's Original Core Values   *42*
On Fire — Culture 2.0   *45*
Why Companies Fail At Culture   *46*
Guiding Principles 2.0 Rollout Process   *47*

4 DELIVER MORE   **57**

Delivering More to Employees (Each Other)   *70*
Delivering More to Customers   *78*
Delivering More to Our Partners   *84*

5 TRANSPARENCY ROCKS   **91**

Start with Questions   *94*
Transparency Rocks Actions   *95*
Ask Anything Initiative   *97*
Why Is Transparency Important?   *102*

6 IMPROVE   **107**

What Needs To Change?   *108*
Why Are We Doing This?   *108*
The Roll Out   *110*
What Did We Change?   *116*
Hire Character First   *130*

7 TAKE RISKS   **141**

What Prevents Us From Taking Risks?   *142*
Why Take Risks?   *144*
What If Taking A Risk Fails?   *150*
What About Marketing?   *151*
The Reward   *156*

8 INCLUDE FUN   **159**

Why Should We Have Fun At Work?   *164*

9 BE HUMBLE   **171**

What Does Being Humble Really Mean?   *171*
The Secret Weapon   *174*
Humility In Action   *176*

10 THE RESULTS   **183**

A Shaved Head   *184*
The Awards   *185*

11 E-COMMERCE CONCEPTS   **189**

12 #ASKANYTHING   **197**

Business Questions   *198*
RealTruck Questions   *202*
Personal Questions   *206*
Misc. Questions   *211*

PRINCIPLES
TO FORTUNE

VISIT:

PrinciplesToFortune.com

SIGN UP:

To Our Newsletter

SHARE:

Take a pic of the book, tag us and share it out

HASHTAG:

#PrinciplesToFortune

CONNECT WITH US SOCIALLY Ⓐ

Facebook.com/principlestofortune

Instagram.com/principlestofortune

Snapchat.com/add/scottbintz

Linkedin.com/in/scottbintz

Twitter.com/bintzness101

WANT AN AUTOGRAPHED COPY?

Order online at ScottBintz.com

FOREWORD

I met Scott Bintz in college. It would turn out to be one of the most reward-ing and beneficial friendships I have had the privilege to be part of. Of course, back then, I didn't know any of that. My first thoughts of Scott were "Man, this guy talks a lot," followed by an observation that he had a generous spirit about him. He is the type of person who genuinely roots for your success and is not envious when it comes. I noticed his propensity for altruism early. I had the good fortune to attend the inaugural ball for the President of the United States. Went out to DC, wore a tux, all kinds of cool stuff. When I got back, Scott had tracked down the school newspaper and con-vinced them to do a story on me, and my time at the event. It was the first of many times that I would benefit from Scott's generosity.

In addition to being close friends, we have also worked together three times. Sometimes that has worked out well for us, like at RealTruck, and others were more learning lessons. Our first time was with a cellular company in the early 90s. Nobody had cell phones. I bet Scott and I were two of the first people in Minot, ND, to rock the handheld brick phone and the bag phone for the car. We were salesmen. Back then you were going after rich people who could afford such a luxury. Try to convince them to sign up on the gold plan which got you 180 minutes a month. Scott was a hard charger, driven to succeed. You would rarely find him at his desk. This was not a good fit for us. Too much competition combined with too much immaturity. I think eventually we came to fisticuffs. So, we parted ways professionally and continued on with life as really good friends.

Scott went on to work for a large manufacturer as their National Sales Manager. It was fun to watch him doing so well. He used to call me from all over the country and we would talk for hours. I was very proud of Scott and not the least bit surprised that he ended up in that position. He was doing his "Scott thing" and working 80 hours a week and the success was following. Eventually Scott had the idea to create a website that sold this manufacturer's product, as well as a few others. I remember when Scott called me from Spokane one night to tell me he was going to start a website, called RealTruck. I didn't think much of it. You have to understand that Scott was always calling with some business idea. So, while it was intriguing that he was trying the internet, it was not that big of a deal. One thing that sets Scott up for success is he is not overly concerned with how things look to others. While many of us have to analyze how this will look, what will people think, what if this fails, Scott is not encumbered with this thought. He bulldozes ahead. So with sheer grit and determination, he grew RealTruck. Eventually, Scott made the decision to go full time on this "basement project".

Meanwhile, I was floundering around, trying to see what kind of a living I could make with a social science degree. Scott asked me to come work for this manufacture and train with him, to take over his job. This time, we were better suited to work together. I learned a ton. We traveled the country setting up deals attempting to help this product go national. Eventually Scott left and I took over. I was now a Director of Sales & Marketing for a fast growing manufacture. Scott was full time at RealTruck, which was keeping its head above water, but just barely. Since RealTruck was one of our accounts, I had a good view on what was going on. I have to admit, there were days, that I thought it might be over for RealTruck and Scott. Other people were starting to catch on to the benefits of e-commerce and it was just a matter of time before someone came along and knocked them out. I point this out to set up the real part of the story.

My days as a big shot Director of Sales and Marketing came to a sudden end; I was terminated. It was devastating. I didn't know where to turn or what to do. I showed up on Scott's doorstep. Scott used to say he wished I could come to work at RealTruck. I would say "I don't think you can afford me Scott." Pride begets the fall. There was no hesitation on Scott's part. While RealTruck was not in a position to hire me, Scott didn't care. I started working there in September of 2007. Our third time working together professionally.

As they say, third time's a charm. One of my immediate contributions was that I could help Scott filter 15 ideas down to a more manageable and attainable 5. Make no mistake, this was not all puppies and rainbows. One day we were "disagreeing" so loud, that our Customer Service Manager came and closed our door and told us we were scaring people. We made a plethora of mistakes. We did a few things right too. And then, we hit gold. Scott had been inspired to improve our company culture. We had toured Zappos and it lit something inside of him. The plane ride home was the quietest Scott has ever been. The real journey starts there and that is the story this book will tell.

All the pieces came together at just the right time. Scott will give plenty of credit to others is this book, rightfully so. It took a village to go on this journey. But let me assure you that while we all had our role to play, Scott was our captain. He was the one who was willing to bet it all on culture and keep our compass facing due North. The one thing I would like to say about this book is; I believe the map we followed can work for anyone. I believe that the principles you try to live by can and should be practiced at work. If you can stay on that path even when it gets turbulent, then I believe that the fortune you seek will come. Whatever that fortune is, let your principles guide you.

—*Jeff Vanlaningham, President of RealTruck 2007-2016*

Scott & Jeff enjoying coffee - 1993

Jeff & Scott still enjoying coffee - 2017

PREFACE

"Time is more value than money.
You can get more money,
but you cannot get more time."
—*Jim Rohn*

T ime is the most valuable thing we have. Have you ever stopped and asked yourself, what am I doing with my time? Am I using it wisely? Since work takes up a good share of our time, we better find or create the kind of workplace we enjoy. In America, the spotlight is on singers, dancers, actors, athletes, and politicians, some with great opinions on business. We seem to care a lot about what they think, say, and do. Some of us follow business. We see, read, and hear about the likes of Elon Musk, Larry Page, Mark Cuban, Richard Branson, Jack Welch, Jeff Bezos, Tony Hsieh, and so forth. I have a great deal of respect and admiration for these entrepreneurs. They are often highly intelligent, went to the absolute best schools, and had access to the best resources. They are big-time calculated risk takers and visionaries. They are the kinds of leaders people seem to naturally want to follow. They built and created some of the best businesses in the world.

As an average guy in business from North Dakota, I don't relate to many of them. Don't get me wrong, I do try to learn from them. I just see them as being way out of my league in so many ways- intelligence, upbringing, education, passion, resources, natural leadership, and so forth. They are clearly first-class people. I, on the other hand, have often felt like a second-class person. It was just me and my mom growing up. She was a waitress and I was a handful. I did poorly in primary school and was often in trouble socially and academically. Having red hair is a real curse when you are young, although it can be a blessing later in life. I eked out a BA in Economics from Minot State University, one of the cheapest colleges in the state. The North Dakota Army National Guard, along with a Pell Grant, helped fund the cost, because I wasn't smart enough or athletic enough to get any scholarships. Clearly, there are a few reasons I don't identify with other well-known entrepreneurs.

WHY READ THIS BOOK?

I am writing this book for a few reasons. First, to share the RealTruck story for those who created it and share how these guiding principles transformed it into unbelievable success. Second, I wrote it for all the entrepreneurs and business folks out there who are like me: not always seen as the smartest in the room, and who don't have access to the best colleges and resources. I wrote it for those who aren't leading or working at the world's greatest or next best "fill in the blank." You know—the rest of us. The normal, average, everyday folks who want to create, build, grow, and learn. The owners, leaders, managers and employees at the 27.9 million[1] small businesses in the U.S. And the future entrepreneurs like me, some of the 20.4 million[2] students attending a regular college or university, who have lots of self-doubt to overcome. And, last, for the cutthroat asshole, profit-first entrepreneurs and executives out there. If your only goal is to get rich, it probably won't fulfill you like you think it will. You will be known and remembered as a cutthroat asshole who got rich. You can change that with principles and create a much more rewarding fortune, which is not just money.

The title of this book is a redirect. The fortune I am referring to is not money. The fortune I am referring to is a combination of experiences, events,

---

1   Source: SBA.Gov
2   Source: NCES National Center For Education Statistics 2017

learnings, insights, and, of course, luck. The real forces behind creating one's fortune are the principles an individual or business lives by. Principles are the external, arbitrary forces that affect human affairs and bring us good or bad fortune. And by good fortune, I don't mean to imply there will not be challenges along the way; rather, good fortune is a series of experiences, not a destination. Some call it chance or luck, but in my experience, good fortune is propelled positively or stifled negatively by the principles we strive to live by. We shape our fortune by our principles.

Living by principles and knowing who you really are (the best or worst parts), along with the hard and soft skills you have (or are willing to put in the time to master), are the basic ingredients for personal or business fortune. Principles can be practiced personally and at work. Often folks have great personal principles but often fall short on them at work. Why? Is it fear? Is it work culture? My experience says it's a mixture of both. This book shares the principles that transformed RealTruck as a business and me as a person.[3]

Little trailer mom and I lived in when I was growing up in the 1980s

---

3   This book is written in context from when I was involved with RealTruck. The principles, policies and business philosophies contained in this book, may or may not currently be practiced at RealTruck. Companies continue to evolve and RealTruck is no exception. This book shares how we changed the business culture and massively grew the company before it was sold to Truck Hero.

1

THE BIG DEAL

"Money and success don't change people;
they merely amplify what is already there."
—*Will Smith*

THE MILLION-DOLLAR CALL

As I was driving, I received word from my banker that the money from the sale of RealTruck® had been wired to my account and I was officially a multimillionaire. It was fucking surreal.

There was a part of me that wanted to just scream and shout, while the other part was calm and shocked. I was amazed, humbled, sad, and happy all at once. It wasn't really the kind of experience you could call someone and say, "Holy shit, dude, I'm a 8-digit millionaire... unbelievable." I thought of my granny; she would have been so proud. I thought of my mother, how hard she worked and sacrificed for me. I thought of my family and how I hoped we wouldn't have to worry about money again.

I had come a long way from the little trailer I grew up in with my single mother, who worked as a waitress to support us. However, my thoughts weren't about going to Disneyland; I wanted to buy my mother a car. It was time for her 2008 Dodge Avenger to get upgraded. I knew her favorite color for a car was red, so in short order I made arrangements to get a red Cadillac SRX, put a big bow on it, asked my mom to lunch, and on the way home made a stop at the dealership. Mom cried, and I felt like a rockstar giving his mom a car. Like a good mom, she thought the car was nicer than what she needed and she was a little worried if I could afford it or not. It was a moment in which I felt I could give a little back to my mom and make her life a little easier. She was so proud. That brought much joy to my heart.

I thought with a certain satisfaction that the company I started in my basement, on its way to a hundred million dollars in sales, was in very good hands. One of the reasons I decided to sell the company was that I felt RealTruck needed a new leader to take it to the next level. Running a $100 million dollar company isn't the same as running a $10 million one. I wanted to put it in good hands to keep it on its mission to "make people's vehicles and lives better" for years to come. I felt like we had proven that by running the business based on our guiding principles, which created a really good work culture in which anything was possible. A good work culture, guided by principles, was clearly having a positive impact on employees, customers, partners, and, of course, the bottom line.

How did we get there? When we were at about 6 million in sales, we bet it all on culture. And that, as it turns out, was the tidal-wave kind of game changer. That was the magic. We failed utterly on our first try on getting principles into our culture and succeeded on our second, more committed attempt. Focusing and enhancing our work culture at RealTruck created the passion and purpose for RealTruck to become an icon for how companies should treat customers, partners, and employees. Lasting e-commerce marketing isn't just a shiny website and slick ads. It's ideas, attitudes, and actions that benefit the customer, the staff, and the brand's business partners. A strategic "way of life" that, when properly executed, creates life-long customers, evangelical employees, helpful partners, and yes, some profit to boot.

Why did we bet it all on culture? When my long-time friend Jeff Vanlaningham came to work for me, he asked me why does RealTruck exist? What makes it different from the 200 other companies that sell pickup accessories online? Why RealTruck? I couldn't answer the question. That really perplexed me. When

Jeff and I were roommates in college, we pondered several things, from how the world should be and what we wanted to do, to what we wanted to experience and what character traits we thought were important to us. One big thing on my list was "to be useful." I wanted to be useful, preferably in a good way. So I asked, how is RealTruck useful? The answers were perhaps decent for some, but were sadly pretty slim for me personally.

We sold pickup accessories to people. We employed people. We had over $6,000,000 in revenue in a single year, which was unbelievable from where we started. Thanks to Justin Deltener, our CTO, and our development team, we had some pretty slick stuff on our website. All pretty cool on the surface. My legacy, I thought, would be that I started a multi-million dollar online store that sold pickup accessories and got rich. For me, this was painfully inadequate. It wasn't very deep in the grand scheme of contribution. Sure, it might be the American dream for some folks, but for me it was a shallow accomplishment in the grand scheme of life. RealTruck was missing something, and so was I.

Money for me has always been a tool needed to get something done, not an end game. I wanted to be able to not worry if I could pay my bills each month. Clearly, for some, money is a motivator, and for others, the desire for it causes them to sacrifice their own values to hang on to it or get more of it. Most people, it seems, have a relationship with money that is rooted in fear, which drives their actions, when fear is really one of the worst motivators. I have certainly had that fear, but money was never my purpose in life. Creating something, yes; building something, yes; doing something I wasn't sure if I could do or not, like running a business, yes. Making a positive impact, yes; employing people and helping their lives be better, yes. But not for the sake of money. Somewhere on my journey I realized that money was like blood to the human body: it was required for life, but not the purpose of it.

At that point, as the self-appointed CEO of RealTruck, I wasn't overly motivated to get up and go to work. What was once fun was now a chore. I would drag myself to work at a company I created and work like a machine to grow the business. Push, pull, drag, get it done.

It was an endless pursuit of more. More sales, more products, more vendors, more employees, more, more, more, but for what? Jeff's questions to me made me question myself and question, why did RealTruck exist? Slowly, I began to realize the reason that work had become a chore and the glamor of building a business from a basement became inadequate was that we didn't really have a purpose except seeking "more". More of this and more of that. I reflected on my life and started with, why do I exist? That answer was clear to me: I exist to be useful to God and the people around me. Since RealTruck was probably the biggest thing available to me, could it have a purpose like that? Could it be more useful? I mean, really, really be useful, not appear useful, but actually help people beyond selling them stuff? Could we run the company by principles rather than by what seemed to be an endless pursuit of more?

Why not? I could be more useful, but how could everyone at RealTruck have a higher mission than selling pickup accessories and earning a paycheck? Jeff had heard of a company called Zappos that was really doing some cool stuff with employees and core values, and they also sold a ton of shoes online. We started reading everything we could about Zappos and their CEO, Tony Hsieh. That year, when we went to the SEMA Show in Las Vegas, we toured Zappos. I somehow came up with the ideal mission for RealTruck: to make people's lives and vehicles better.

If we could get the culture right, get principles driving the business, everything else would work out. And it did. However, it did not happen overnight, and there were some definite bumps in the road.

Our first attempt failed. We had core values that Jeff and I wrote, printed on fancy paper, and handed out. No one embraced them as we had anticipated they would. Heck, most of our employees couldn't even tell you what they were. I was baffled.

I brought them up in meetings, but we weren't successful at really getting these values accepted or practiced. We did successfully define RealTruck's mission: to make people's lives and vehicles better. This we carried to future iterations of our values.

We definitely fell short of being really committed to principles that supported that mission. From Zappos we learned about the books *Good to Great* by Jim
Collins, *Tribal Leadership* by Dave Logan, John King, and Halee Fischer-Wright,
and *Peak: How Great Companies Get Their Mojo* from Maslow by Chip Conley. I
devoured these books. I thought, if Tony could do it at Zappos, maybe, just
maybe, we could do it at RealTruck. When Tony's book *Delivering Happiness* came
out in 2010, it helped connect the dots between those other three books.

I was next-level inspired. Those four books would become the "core"
books I wanted anyone working at RealTruck to read. On my time or theirs.
Whatever it took. I handed them out like candy at a parade. We scrapped our
first core values and started over.

On our second attempt to reinvent our core values as guiding principles
driving RealTruck, we started with finding out the values of our employees
and grouped them. These new groups of personal values became the basis
for RealTruck's new guiding principles. We, the leaders of the company—Jeff,
Justin, and I—had to be 100% committed to principles first. We would hire, fire,
reward, and recognize using them as the standard. Once we developed them,
and as we rolled them out one by one, I would send out an email, and all the
departments would have meetings about them.

How can we practice them? Where are we not practicing them? Why should
we practice them? We want to practice these principles in everything we do.
We will hire, reward, and recognize by them. If you have them, or want to have
them, then RealTruck will be a great place to work and grow professionally. If
you don't have or want to practice them, then it will not.

One by one, these principles became integrated into RealTruck's culture.
Practicing these principles and focusing on culture changed everything for me
personally and for RealTruck. It was amazing to be a part of it. To get a front
row seat to what was to come. We had a positive impact on our employees
beyond a job, on our customers beyond just selling them stuff, and with our
partners beyond just buying stuff from them. RealTruck became a super fun
place to work. Customers and partners loved and praised us. We were doing

something really special. Other companies would come for a tour and ask us for advice. Customers would write us sharing their experience with something special a customer service rep had done for them, like sending flowers for their birthday. Some would even call and want a signed RealTruck T-shirt. Not autographed from me but from the CS team. Our vendor partners would visit and later share that it was the most fun business trip they had ever taken, and they certainly didn't expect that from a trip to North Dakota.

UPS, one of our great partners, featured us in brochures and even included us in a national ad campaign. It was exhilarating and so very emotionally rewarding. We had holiday parties that were so fun, they were remembered for years to come. It was something that had value beyond just making money. It had purpose, personality, and passion.

Often, I felt unworthy and unqualified to be the guy leading such a great thing. Wasn't this something that someone smarter, more qualified, more organized, more charismatic would be leading? Not me—I was the kid from the trailer park who never met his father. Fortunately for me, I had really qualified, high-character, smart folks around me. Often I get a lot of praise for Real-Truck's rags-to-riches success. But that praise really belongs to all the folks at RealTruck. Great companies don't occur because of one person. And Real-Truck's success didn't occur because of me. It was all about the people and the company culture we built together.

This book shares how we went from a small, little-known e-commerce company to a mega e-commerce superstore with an amazing company culture. How we changed RealTruck from an online pickup accessories store without purpose to an e-commerce company on a mission to make people's lives better, which just happened to become a superstore for pickup accessories.

My mom and her new wheels

" *I had a front row seat for the transformation of RealTruck. The way Scott pulled together all of our collective values and formed our Guiding Principles was magical. But the real inspiration was what happened when we truly started living by those principles. We became a different company."*
—Jeff Vanlaningham

HOW THE HELL DID YOU GET THERE?

*"Success is no accident. It is hard work, perseverance,
learning, studying, sacrifice, and, most of all,
love of what you are doing or learning to do."*
—Pele, World-Renowned Soccer Player

Well, that's the main purpose of this book. To share how principles first changed the work culture and rocketed RealTruck, a little company from North Dakota, from a basement duplex to $100+ million in sales, all while having a good time and delivering more to customers, employees, and partners.

How did a company from rural North Dakota, with no money or Ivy League employees, with workers who didn't ever actually touch a product, become the #1 place online to get pickup accessories?

T-shirt signed by
Customer Service Team

UPS brochure

How did an e-commerce company that happened to sell pickup accessories from the little state of North Dakota…

- Be awarded BizRate's Platinum Circle of Excellence for multiple years
- Get North Dakota Young People's Top 3 Best Places to Work for multiple years
- Be featured in National Ads by UPS
- Process over 90% of orders automatically
- Ship 95% of Orders sooner than expected
- Become 100% drop ship
- Have virtually no debt
- Be named Prairie Business Best 50 Places to Work
- Get the Innovation Award from the Information Technology Council of North Dakota
- Be named Vendor of The Year for multiple vendors and years
- Receive the Growing Jamestown Award
- Be named Internet Retailers Top 300 Mobile
- Be named Internet Retailers Top 500
- Be named Internet Retailers 8 Fastest Growing Mobile
- Be named Internet Retailers 14th Fastest Growing in Top 500
- Be named IRCE Mobile Commerce Excellence Award contender alongside Lancôme (who won), eBay, and Wayfair

The short answer is: guiding principles and work culture.

The next chapter is about bucking the norm, innovation, and my journey to starting RealTruck and getting it going in the early days. If you are excited to learn about how we got the culture rocking at RealTruck, then jump to the Creating Culture chapter.

. . .

Breakfast with the some of the team at the SEMA Show 2015

Some of the Fargo team getting ready to do a "dance" video

Chad Bolte and Shawn Herrick having some fun at the SEMA Show

2
AGAINST THE WIND

"We were runnin' against the wind

We were young and strong, we were runnin' against the wind

Well I'm older now and still runnin'

Against the wind."

—Bob Seger

Entrepreneurs and great businesses are always going against the wind. If you are in business, no matter what goal or journey you decide to pursue, you are always going to meet resistance and find yourself moving against the wind. In order to change, improve, or innovate, you will find yourself going against the flow of the status quo.

For example, before I started RealTruck, I worked as a manufacturer's rep for a company that represented about fifteen pickup truck accessory and equipment manufacturers. I was always searching for better and more efficient ways to do things. As I was calling on dealers, I was sure there had to be an easier way to sell products. This was at a time when ordering through the Internet was just beginning. I placed my first order on Staples.com, and I was quite impressed that my order showed up at my house a few days later.

One of the products my company represented at the time, Northwest Representation, Inc., was the Access® roll-up cover made by Agri-Cover, Inc. We set up dealers across the northwest United States and also attended retailer and industry trade shows. I would call on pickup accessories stores and show them the products we represented, from snow plows to pickup bed covers from various manufacturers around the United States. If they liked our products, we signed them up as a dealer and then NW Reps would get paid a commission on the sales from those dealers in a given geographical area (often referred to as independent agents, manufacturer agents, or manufacturer representatives). At the retail trade shows- boat, car, sport shows and so forth- we would show products and then refer consumers to the local dealers we had set up to buy whatever product they were interested in. This was a lot of work, and I thought there had to be a way to speed up the process. For the pickup bed cover we offered at the time, we felt the only way to sell the bed cover was to show it on a pickup. Roll it open and roll it closed. We decided to try a new approach to marketing by creating a television commercial.

TV OR TRADE SHOWS

I thought TV was a way to "show the product" and not have to attend 50 trade shows a year. Our hope was that we could sell more covers and mitigate our cost while increasing our sales. TV was seen as a marketing tool for large companies, but somehow I managed to talk Agri-Cover and three of their dealers into funding the TV commercial. It was a lot of fun to make the commercial, although some doubted a 30-second spot would work. Splitting the cost four ways lowered the financial risk and with a little persuasion, we tried it. The TV commercial was a success and we sold a lot more Access covers. The financial risk paid off.

This got me thinking about getting someone to build a website. What if we built a website, somehow converted the TV ad to a video, and put that on the site and set it up so you could order? Again, e-commerce was the wild west at that time. I asked Agri-Cover and they didn't want to do it. I asked the three dealers, and they didn't want to do it. I started trying to convince the brick-and-mortar pickup accessory stores that this was the way of the future and a new vertical for revenue for their stores. I had no success. None.

Then I decided, what if I do it? I had a friend going to college for web development. He needed some extra cash for college, so maybe he would be willing to build it? My plan was to get a website built, then show my pickup accessory accounts that it worked and they could sell online. If I could do it, then they certainly could do it, as they had more resources than I did. If we could sell more products, then I could stop attending trade shows. I asked Agri-Cover if it was alright to try my little experiment, and to my surprise they said sure, but at my expense. And so the RealTruck.com story began...

REALTRUCK BEGINS

My initial vision to get the factory and the brick-and-mortar stores to set up websites to sell their products was unsuccessful. They did not want to pay for and put resources behind the development of websites. They were focused on their right-now business and not the future. But none of us really had any idea how enormously crazy big that selling on the Internet would become.

RealTruck.com initially was just going to be a prototype to show brick-and-mortar stores and pickup accessory manufacturers in order to get them to sell their products online. I was terribly unsuccessful convincing most of them. I did convince a few, but they would not provide the resources to make it successful, or they would put up a website with few products, no online checkout, and a big phone number to call to place the order. Meanwhile at RealTruck headquarters, which was the basement of a duplex, I kept trying to push the bar by adding products to the website. The original three products were the Access® roll-up cover, the Pop and Lock® tailgate lock, and the Bedrug® bedliner.

RealTruck begins in basement 1998

THE BEST QUALIFIED TO SELL ONLINE

Even though the manufacturers, wholesalers, and pickup truck accessories stores were more well-equipped to be successful selling online—they had better resources in terms of money, people, products, business experience, experts in their area—they lacked two essential ingredients: open-mindedness and passion. It was up to my little rep firm to take up the task of selling pickup accessories online.

Any time there is a new road or network to connect people, it will always shift business, whether you agree with it or not. The postal service made way for the Sears catalog and other mail order companies. The interstate road systems made way for big box retail stores. TV made way for the Home Shopping Network and other TV shopping channels. The Internet made way for e-commerce companies such as Amazon and RealTruck. The mobile phone is now the newest network connecting people in ways never seen before.

When you're going against the direction of the current business wind, you have to accept you're not going to win a popularity contest. And most of the feedback you get will be around why it "won't" work. It's like a little train with not much of an engine, but get that engine going in a certain direction and slowly more and more people will get on board. Not everyone will board your train. They don't like the train, they don't think it will work, or they think it's a waste of time. Others may hop on but then jump off because it's going too slow and they can't see where it's going to take them. The more people get on board, the stronger the engine becomes.

Most game-changing ideas are not accepted right away. And often those best able to capitalize on them won't. This is because of what Jim Collins covers in masterly detail in his book Good to Great. You will not be great if you deny the brutal facts of the market situation. Jumping on a new road, for me, was life changing.

THE BRUTAL FACTS

Don't think for a minute life is like a Monopoly game, where you roll the dice and if you work hard, you will be rewarded fairly. That may have been true at one time, but not anymore. Don't get me wrong, you can be successful, but don't kid yourself about how the board of life is set up. Starting like I did with a single mom who was a waitress living in a trailer park, you quickly realize a few things.

In the real world, all the properties and resources are already owned by other people, often for generations. If you're just starting like I did, you probably only have one die to roll with most the numbers missing. Others may have 6 and 7 complete dice to roll. Some even have dice with a six on every side.

When I went past go, I'd get five bucks when others were getting 100 bucks and others 1,000 bucks. This doesn't mean you can't overcome adversity; it just means you need to be aware of the brutal facts of the situation. You can't get better at the game if you don't know all the rules and pitfalls. This means it's even more important to master skills, find mentors, and take risks. Skills have value, especially if others know what you have in your toolbelt. Mentors can speed up the learning curve and help you develop skills faster. This new network, the Internet, along with my willingness to risk it with really nothing to lose, is what changed the Monopoly game of life.

OBSTACLES AND MORE OBSTACLES

I had to overcome some obstacles before I officially started RealTruck. I chatted with my buddy who was going to school for web development. He was ready to jump on, and we figured out his hourly pay. He started part-time with the goal of getting an online store set up. To do this, we needed to get an Internet connection at his apartment and my house. At the time, dial-up was the only option we knew of. We needed a domain name, hosting, and email. My friend called around and asked me to meet him at an attorney's office. We met, and the dial-up Internet and hosting company was conveniently located in a unused back room of the attorney's office. It was a bit sketchy. We told the owner of the Internet provider company our plans, and that we needed dial-up and server hosting. He asked what is now an obvious question: What was the name of company domain we wanted? Shit, I hadn't even thought of one. The dial-up guy started rattling off ideas. One of them was RealTruck.

About three months into the project, my website guy called and said the server is gone. No dial-up, no hosting. Thankfully he had a backup of everything. We panicked, shot up to the attorney's office, and went to the back room to find nothing there. He had bolted. However, he must have originally wanted to be a straight shooter, because when he registered the domain RealTruck, he registered it to me. We found another dial-up and hosting company and continued development.

The next hurdle was to set up credit card processing. This almost killed the deal. First, for a virtual store at the time, it was almost impossible to explain what kind of business we were planning on doing. Selling online was new. Virtual stores were unheard of. You don't have a storefront? You don't stock any product? How are you going to have customers? How are you going to swipe their card? We finally found a credit card processor, but I had to sign a three-year lease at $40/month. This delayed things for about a week as I pondered it. I thought, what if everyone is right and we don't sell anything? I'll have this stupid $40/month payment for three years, which I couldn't really afford at the time. Clearly, you know the decision I made. I signed up for the manual credit card processing machine, which had to be plugged into a telephone line to work, also costing another $50/month.

A few months later, in November 1998, the website was published. We had a home page, three product pages, a cart, and checkout process along with a video loaded on the website of the TV commercial we made. It looked badass (at the time).

As good fortune would have it, that evening RealTruck got its first sale. A gentleman from the great state of Tennessee ordered an Access cover for his short bed 1997 Ford F150. This created another dilemma. I technically didn't

RealTruck website 1998

have accounts with the manufacturers to order any of the three products the site offered. I printed the order from the website and "purged" it. None of the manufacturers or wholesalers really had much for email at the time. Everything was done via fax or phone. If they did have an email, it was on one computer, everyone in the company used it, and it was checked maybe once a week. I manually keyed in the credit card number into my shiny new credit card processing machine, it dialed and captured the funds. The next morning I called Chuck, one of the owners of Agri-Cover, Inc., and asked if I could set up a buying account with him. He said yes. So, on a Word document, I wrote up the purchase order along with the ship-to address and faxed the order in. Agri-Cover shipped it via UPS using the same fax and faxed back tracking information. I then re-typed the tracking number into the email, thanked the customer for ordering, and included the tracking number. Holy smokes. This was crazy cool. That seemed pretty automated at the time.

My next problem was I didn't really know anything about accounting. I knew the credit card processor was going to put the funds into my bank account in a few days and Agri-Cover would be mailing a bill due in 30 days. I didn't realize it at the time, but this would be a big ingredient in being able to grow as fast as our operations could keep up with things. Get paid in 4-5 days and not have to pay the product cost for 30 days. Later, most suppliers would let you pay in 10 days and get a 2% discount. Over time, we realized we could grow as fast as we could sell, process orders, and post tracking.

I called a friend from college, Keith, who was my only 4.0 GPA friend, and asked him if he would do the books to start. He said yes. Keith lived in a different town, so each week I would mail him all the orders and bills.

I didn't realize it at the time, but I was picking up another awareness. You can't do everything and be good at it. Focus on what you are good at and let others help you with what you are not good at. I'm more of a risk taker and a get-it-done kind of person, not a money organizer or planner. Not once did I wish to know how to web develop or do accounting. Often folks are shocked to find out that I don't know how to do web development. When it comes to web development, I'm more wired to connect dots and ideas and then knock down mental or physical obstacles that stand in the way of someone else being able to write code and turn that idea into reality. My favorite thing to say to developers is, "Don't tell me we can't do it. We put a man on the moon in 1969. What we are doing can't be that hard."

RealTruck grew very slowly. An order would come in every other day or so. I would repeat the ordering process and direct my developer friend to do things to make the website better. At that time, only a web developer could do anything to the website from adding products to making improvements.

CHANGING THE MARKET

To add products, there were two big obstacles:
1. A web developer doesn't like to do it; they prefer to do cool code stuff.
2. If you have no money to stock products, you have to find and convince partners like manufacturers or wholesalers to set up an account for a "virtual" store and drop ship for you, then send back tracking.

My web guy reluctantly added products as I was able to find manufacturers that would drop ship, which was a long and slow process. Often, they didn't even have access to images for their products except to mail a printed catalog and price guide. I was still trying to convince the pickup truck accessory stores to sell online, and I even offered to let them clone the RealTruck website. Even with RealTruck having a little success with sales, most were not interested. For the companies that were interested, we cloned the RealTruck website and we provided them training and support. The problem was that none of them put any time, effort, or resources into making the site work for their company. If they did authorize an employee to work on it, it would be the person with the least authority and with the understanding that everything else is more important. Or at least that is how it seems to me.

As for finding more products, that was challenging. Most manufacturers we approached were very sure selling online would not work. No one is going to buy something they can't touch from a company they have never heard of. You can sell staplers online, but not pickup accessories. I would share with them that we were having a little success selling online. They came up with all sorts of excuses why online selling would not work for their products. Most looked at a website as a marketing brochure. Some would build websites and not update them for five years. Even when faced with my sales data, they would deny the facts. If I was able to get by that, the next obstacle was they felt it would take away from local dealer business or their current mail-order dealers.

A big manufacturer might have 1,000 dealers and a smaller one 100 dealers. I would point out that with 35,000 or so cities in the U.S., even with 1,000 dealers there were huge gaps. The belief was that mail-order catalog companies were covering that gap. Some companies had convinced themselves that their customers would drive 100 miles to buy their product. Even then I couldn't imagine someone driving 100 miles for a pair of nerf bars. I would try to convince them that not everyone would drive to get products and that some folks might appreciate buying it online and having it show up to their door. They were also sure that the number of people who would buy a product and install it themselves was minimal and also covered by mail-order companies.

I kept at it and very, very slowly a manufacturer would say sure, let's give it a try. Those more open-minded companies would, ten years later, see e-commerce companies like RealTruck and Auto Anything™ making up a good share of their top 10 accounts. As for mail order, like brick-and-mortar stores, those companies often struggled with getting online and doing it right. They were too focused on their now business, which was mail order. In reality, if the JC Whitney® and Stylin Trucks of the world at that time had got going on this "new people connecting network," the Internet, they would be light years ahead. But as luck would have it, they didn't, and that gave RealTruck lots of time to find partners and figure things out.

Once we were able to convince a pickup accessory manufacturer to let us sell their products, that led to more changes. No one had digital product images, videos, or even product data. It was all on printed brochures and printed application guides. Often, whoever created the printed brochure for the manufacturer didn't have a way to get the digital files they had to you. It could take a month to get whomever designed the printed literature to put it on a CD and mail it to us. We would take pictures of the brochures and load that, along with typing out the application guides in a manner that was conducive for online orders.

I spent most of my evenings searching the Internet and submitting the RealTruck website to directories, search engines, and forums. At the time there were what seemed like hundreds of search engines and literally thousands and thousands of specialty directories on the web, from state directories and hobby directories to industry and personal directories. It kept me busy for what seemed like months and months, but that helped folks find us online. Often the submission process was glitchy, so I would have to submit the same form ten times. I would type out all the info, our address, what we sold, etc., click submit, and the site would wipe it out. And at that time, some of the forms to add your site had a hundred questions. It seemed crazy, but every time I submitted Real-Truck to a directory, I felt like things were gonna be alright.

I shared my findings with some of my pickup accessory store accounts, especially the few that had websites, with regards to products, submitting to search engines, and directories for web traffic. Again, most would not put in the work. What would spending fifteen minutes adding a site to one web directory do in the big scheme of things, anyways? For some reason, I was very passionate that it was what was best. Little steps is how you climb a mountain. One step after another. Little hits rather than swinging for the fence. Little action after little action would add up over time. When Google started to become the number-one search engine, followed by Yahoo and MSN, since we had thousands of listings on all those specialty directories and forums, we ranked better in the bigger search engines.

We kept selling a little more and a little more, adding new products occasionally. In May 2000, I decided to sell Northwest Representation to Greg Hoff, the sale rep who worked for me at the time. He would take over NW Reps and I would continue RealTruck as my little hobby business. We set up a deal and he bought me out over the course of three years. I took a job again for Agri-Cover, Inc., as their national sales manager.

That job kept us afloat personally, and I used the money I was getting from Greg each month to enhance the RealTruck website. We had enough business coming in that I began to hire employees to process orders. This continued from May 2000 until May 2003. We added products, sales increased, we hired more employees, and everything we made went into making the RealTruck website better. In 2003, we had about five employees.

FULL-TIME REALTRUCK

As RealTruck grew, my day job became more challenging. A lot of the accounts Agri-Cover had looked at RealTruck as a competitor. "Your national sales manager is competing with us." We didn't see it that way. We saw that often someone would learn about the Access roll-up cover via RealTruck and the Internet. Some would buy it online, which was good for Agri-Cover and RealTruck.

Others would print off the product from the RealTruck website, take it to a pickup accessory store, and that store would call Agri-Cover and ask to become a dealer. In that case it was good for Agri-Cover and good for expanding the popularity of the Access roll-up cover. Agri-Cover was starting to sign dealers from all around the country. At that time Agri-Cover was strong in the Great Plains states and in the northwest but spotty everywhere else. That changed rapidly.

The Internet helped Agri-Cover get new dealers via finding their products on RealTruck and on the Agri-Cover website. RealTruck ranked way better and had more products, which was a bigger funnel for exposing folks to the products we had online. RealTruck was also getting some sales with those customers daring enough to buy online. In addition, the future sales for Agri-Cover directly from these new dealers from around the country was pretty sweet since they did not have the expense of a sales rep visiting them in person. I could tell it was getting to be too much to explain that to Agri-Cover's dealers. RealTruck was getting bigger, and I needed to be there full time. I owe a great debt of gratitude to Chuck and Steve, the owners of Agri-Cover, for the employment opportunity, helping me start Northwest Representation, hiring me as the their national sales manager, supporting me with RealTruck, teaching me about business, and so much more.

During that time, another great thing happened. I was introduced to Mind Tremors, a web development company in Fargo, ND, owned by Justin and Joshua Deltener, who are also twins. They became the web developers for RealTruck moving forward. Justin's wife, Kelly, was the project manager, Josh tended to do graphics and network stuff, and Justin did the heavier web development, although both could pretty much do it all. This is when we really stepped up our web development game.

Now that I was at RealTruck full time, it was really important we grow, since my family and employees were counting on me to make payroll twice a month. This increased the need to team up with more manufacturers. Even in 2003, five years later, it was still difficult to convince a manufacturer to let us sell their products online and have them drop ship the orders.

In the automotive industry, the big show of the year is in November and it's called the SEMA (Specialty Equipment Marketing Association) show. I started going there when I worked at Agri-Cover as a factory rep before I had my manufacturers' rep firm, NW Reps. At Agri-Cover, I would not have been able to foresee I would be attending the show every year for the next 25 years.

At the SEMA Show, manufacturers exhibited their products. Wholesalers, local dealers and mail order companies in the automotive space would attend the show to see the manufacturers they were doing business with and to find new products to offer their customers. The automotive aftermarket is a big industry, and the show is massive, from spark plugs and batteries to rims and pickup bed covers. Pickup accessories were probably one of the smaller areas of the show at the time. But it was growing, and so was RealTruck.

At this time, we also had a printed catalog. We did this because it made us appear less virtual, more like a mail-order company than an e-commerce company. That made finding new vendors a little easier.

There was also a sentiment developing with the manufacturers that e-commerce companies were giving away products and discounting too much. The popular opinion was that e-commerce companies had no overhead, so they just "whored-up" street pricing and sold everything for just a little above cost. Certainly some companies selling online were big discounters, and most of those would eventually go broke. I had learned at Agri-Cover there was an art between balancing volume and margin. I also had learned that profitability is directly tied to how well you buy. Meaning, the street price is the street price, and you can't really control that for a product; the market does. If you have really great service and really great delivery, perhaps you can be a little more expensive than the street price as people will pay a little more for better service—but not a lot. So the best way to improve profit is to buy better and take advantage of early pay discounts, rebate programs, advertising co-op dollars, and so forth. One thing overlooked by the manufacturers regarding e-commerce companies was that they did have overhead, but it was a different kind. We didn't have inventory costs or nice-looking storefront costs. However, we did have web development expenses and marketing expenses.

You can't live in North Dakota selling all over the U.S. without some marketing going on. Web development was our largest expense. We were putting virtually all of our profits into improving the website. We were often going into debt with creative "leases" for software development, maxing our lines of credit at the bank and, at one time, selling just about everything I owned and turning my house, RealTruck, and what seems like my life over to a banker to keep RealTruck going.

We probably had about a million dollars into website development at that point. I always looked at it a certain way: if an enhancement to our website cost $25,000, $50,000, or even $100,000 at the time, the improvement from whatever module, widget, program, or automation we developed would benefit us for years. If it created more efficiency operationally, more traffic or a higher conversion rate, then it was a good investment to make. Unfortunately—or perhaps, in my case, fortunately—we had limited resources, so we had to choose our improvements wisely and make sure they were successful to get our future return on investment.

Because of Justin and Josh Deltener, we were really doing some cool stuff. We set it up so people could add products to the website. During the SEMA show, I would meet with potential vendors (manufacturers), show them the printed catalog, and show them our website on my oversized laptop (Justin liked big laptops; often traveling people joked that they didn't realize Commodore 64 made laptops). I'd explain that we wouldn't "over" discount, that we could grow their product and grow the market, that we paid our bills on time, and that if they set us up with good pricing without having to buy inventory, it would be a good deal for both of us. With good images, product information, and easy-to-understand order controls, we could sell their product without someone touching or seeing it in person. A few would say sure, let's give it a try.

A few times I offered a bet. If a vendor was on the fence, I would say, "Tell you what, I'll go back to my hotel room tonight and add your product to our site, and if we sell one online before the show is over, then you will set us up as a dealer. If we don't sell one, then I won't bug you for another year, and I'll send you a good book to read from Amazon." If they agreed, I'd snap some pictures of their products on display with my digital camera, grab their printed literature and application guide and, thanks to Justin and Josh's product line editor, even I, with no web coding skills, could quickly add the products to the website. As good fortune would have it, I never lost the bet.

For some of the earlier products we were selling, RealTruck was starting to be on the top 10 account list for those manufacturers. That was pretty cool. Who would have thought? We grew every year. Sold more, hired more people, invested more in development.

Often I wondered if I was really qualified to lead RealTruck. It was growing rapidly. Was I qualified? Could I find someone who would do it better?

At this time, my long-time friend Jeff Vanlaningham was working for another company. Out of college he landed a job at Kraft Foods, then went on to Merck. When I had decided to leave Agri-Cover, I told Chuck he had to meet Jeff and should hire him to replace me. He did. Personally, I had always wanted to hire Jeff. I didn't want to hire him away from a big battleship onto my little boat, which could sink a lot easier. Then, as he mentioned in the foreword of this book, he lost his job and wanted to get working right away. I wanted to hire him badly. He was a seeker. Always learning something new and then eager to share that with everyone.

There was the time he started learning about colognes. I mean, he went deep: oils, fragrances for this and that, which last longer, which works better for each season, this president wore this cologne, on and on. But I noticed he left a trail of guys smelling better in his wake. He's very insightful, and one of the funniest guys you will ever meet. He also has a great marketing eye, even though he never went to school for that.

But there was a problem, I could only afford to pay him about half what he was making, and RealTruck was no Merck. If a big wave hit us, we would be fish food. He signed up. This would be another ingredient for our future success.

Now I realize, some people say don't hire friends. I was kind of on the fence about it at the time. I was on a flight to Alaska on my way to an event and pondered this question. Should you hire a friend? Like a lightning bolt it struck me. We spend 40 or more hours of our life every week working, for what could be the next 40 years. I decided right then I'd prefer to do that with people I like. Now, that doesn't mean everyone I like would work well with me. It just means if there is a fit, I'd go with who I like. Later I would notice I tended to hire folks based on two main things, trust and character. Could I trust them, and what is their character like? Skills can be learned or taught fairly easy. Trust and character, on the other hand, not so much.

I learned that if you can get the right people in the right spots, work becomes easier. One of Jeff's many qualities is that he is able to focus, which is a challenge for me. I want to do a hundred things all at the same time and have them all done yesterday. When I read the book *Steve Jobs* by Walter Isaacson, I painfully identified with the reality distortion field (RDF). I seem to have a similar trait. I was really good for removing obstacles and pushing people to get things done, but also very taxing on them. When they would say it will be done in a month, I'd say, no, we will have it done Friday.

As RealTruck grew, having a hundred important things that needed to be done by Friday wasn't realistic, Jeff would tell me. Jeff would pin me down and ask what were the three most important things we needed to do. He'd say, let's focus on those. You can still have your list of 100, but let's get folks having a top three in each department. It made sense, but I did have a tendency to turn the three we agreed on into six or nine from time to time.

This is when I started realizing more and more that not all people are going to be good at everything. If you have a customer service manager that is great at rah rah, fun, and creating a great customer experience, they may suck at employee discipline. If they are great at employee discipline and lack the rah rah skills, they may not have any employees still working. It's better to amplify what you are good at and let others help with what you are not good at.

I began to realize this idea applies to me, but it also needed to apply to everyone else. I'm really good at seeing patterns. I would get so mad when others around me couldn't see what I see. For instance, wanting a hundred things done at the same time, I expected everyone to be good at everything. Good at customer service, order fulfillment, vendor negotiations, managing, adding products, coming up with development ideas, improving processing, making decisions, taking calculated risks, being open-minded, editing images and video, understanding search engine optimization, calculating margin, and so on. Everyone had to be masters of all the hard and soft skills.

Thanks to Jeff, I know that this is not a realistic expectation and I'm setting people up for failure. I began to realize what was easy for me to see didn't mean it was easy for everyone else to see. That is where trust comes in to bridge the gap. It meant I needed to look for things people are good at rather than always focusing on what they are not.

Jeff started as RealTruck's first vice president and went on to become president. Justin Deltener was our first direct hire web developer who would go on to be our CTO (chief technical officer). Those two gentlemen became my best fans, best critics, best advisors, and best evangelists for RealTruck.

We were growing like crazy. We built a new facility with 14,000 square feet of warehouse space and 12,000 square feet of office space. I had the idea that if we warehoused some of the products, we could ship them faster and make a little more money. I think I thought since we figured out e-commerce and running a company, adding a warehouse would be no harder. This decision about killed us. First, it was expensive, and second, we had no idea how to run a warehouse. I thought if we built it, the right person would come along and magically optimize warehouse operations. That didn't happen.

For returns, we had always shipped them back to where we ordered them from, which was easy to get the return credit one product at a time. With a warehouse, vendors expected us to take returns back ourselves and then every few months, put them on a pallet and ship that back. A few issues with this: First, vendors were good about one-at-a-time credits. When there was $5,000 of returns on a pallet, they weren't the best at giving a full credit because it seemed like a lot at once. Second, returns piled up and they were hard to keep organized. For inventory management, even if we had $25,000 of stock for a given brand, we still had to drop ship most of the orders and we never seemed to have the right items in stock. Plus with pickup accessories, you have big items, small items, and everything in between. One product, such as a chrome bug shield, might have 200 individual parts to fit various year, make, and model of vehicles. So we rarely had the right one in stock.

When you organize the stock in the warehouse, do you do it by brand? Or by product category? We had no idea. What's the best way to rotate the stock? UPS was great at hooking us up with the technology we needed to run a warehouse, but we just didn't have any of the skills and talents to properly take advantage of it. Plus with new vendors, since we had a warehouse, they would want us to order $10,000 or $20,000 of stock as an opening order and then drop ship what we didn't have in stock, which greatly slowed down onboarding new vendors as we could only afford so much inventory. It was a crazy time. It was a difficult and challenging time.

This was further compounded when our industry had its first huge kick in the pants. In 2007, new pickup sales started to slow and gas prices[4] went through the roof. The market rapidly contracted. Fewer new pickups sold means less pickup accessories sold. Over the next couple of years, pickup sales continued to drop. Pickup sales would eventually drop 50%[5] to what they were. How would we survive if our sales got cut in half? We saw sales starting to slow and we needed to get in a position to survive the downturn.

Jeff said, we are good at marketing online, good at automating the drop ship process, and good at customer service. Let's stop trying to be great at everything. We decided to sell the facility and move into one that just had an office space. As luck would have it, a building supply company wanted to set up shop in town. Rather than build, they bought the facility. We took a loss on it, but it saved us big time on cash flow. Plus, having better focus on the three things rather than everything, we spent more time looking for partners that fit

---

4   2007 Record High Gas Prices Source: http://money.cnn.com/2007/05/06/news/economy/gasoline/

5   Vehicle Historical Report Source: http://www.macrotrends.net/1372/auto-and-light-truck-sales-historical-chart

our business model. That model was drop ship only. We looked at the numbers from when we had a warehouse, and it was true that because of stocking we were able to buy products about 5% cheaper. However, running a warehouse along with the cost of inventory turnover costs us way more than 5%.

We had always been a reasonably transparent company. I shared that we were in for some tough times and we needed to tighten our belts to survive as we were starting to lose money. We needed to watch our spending, especially on marketing. We needed to cut costs anywhere we could, and that might even be payroll. Crunching the numbers, it looked like we needed to cut payroll by about 25%. I was sick to my stomach. I have never liked telling someone to take their ball and play elsewhere. Someone who enjoys letting someone go should never be in a position to do so, in my opinion. I absolutely hate it. Besides running the company effectively, later I would learn the best solution for not being put in a position to let someone go is to hire well. If someone wants to go, then I'd like to be in a position to help them get to where they want to go. Nobody likes rejection and nobody likes being told "their services" were no longer needed. I certainly didn't like to be the one saying it.

This 25% reduction was a problem. The thought of laying off an employee was akin to telling a family member they had to go. What were we going to do? Jeff, Justin, and I had many conversations on it. Ultimately we decided upper management would need to take a 30% pay cut, front line managers a 10% pay cut. On the front lines, such as customer service, returns, and order fulfillment, there would be, no pay cuts. Those in management and upper management were in a better position to take the hit. To those whom much is given, much is expected.

We were very transparent with everyone in the company on what was going on in the company and in the marketplace. We hoped these would be temporary cuts but didn't know for sure. One manager left; taking a 10% pay cut was just too much, and he felt it was unfair. It was a good thing. This person was highly skilled. An individual rock star—falling into the classification of *I would not hire them again*, because they felt smarter and more important than everyone else. They didn't want any kind of personal sacrifice for the company's problems.

They would not have fit into the culture that was to come.

So what happened with rapid market downturn and the cost cutting? I had to max out our lines of credit, sell just about everything I had, and sign my life away to a banker, along with my house, to extend our credit line. Some e-commerce companies went broke. Manufacturers were raising prices. Shipping costs increased. It was nip and tuck for awhile. As for RealTruck, we saw cost decreases and efficiency increases everywhere from the electric bill to automating some of the accounting processing. We became more efficient operationally by leaps and bounds. We got better at answering the phone faster. We couldn't afford to pay any overtime and had to make do. Even though the number of pickups sold was decreasing, our sales kept growing and growing.

Eventually, our profitability was greater than expected. Everyone who took pay cuts returned to their original pay, and many got raises. We had company-wide bonuses and raised the base wage of the front lines. How did this happen with such a huge market downturn? It was a glimpse of what was to come. If you take care of employees, they will step up and make sacrifices for the good of their coworkers and the company.

THE RACETRACK

It was an exciting time of growth, learning, doing things we didn't think we could do. Learn how to lead more effectively. More customers, more employees, more partners. But it seemed like we were missing something. I was missing something. Even though we were starting to kill it in a business sense, I was starting to have to drag myself to work. It was losing its fun. My passion for business was fading. In trying to create some excitement personally, I got into circle track racing on dirt as a way to blow off steam and relax.

I know what you are thinking: how can driving a dirt track race car into a corner at 75 mph be relaxing? I'm not totally sure, but I do know it calms the mind down to a single thought when you are racing: How am I going to drive this car around the corner without blowing it off the track, running into another car, or worse yet, hitting a wall? It was a new challenge. I didn't know anything about fixing cars or racing. I'm not a very mechanical person. Growing up, we had a hammer and silverware we used to fix things.

There are many lessons I learned in business and racing that seemed to help each other. Like in business, unless you are naturally gifted, the three biggest things you need are persistence, determination, and open-mindedness. You also need some luck or good fortune. Just like in business, those who feel more lucky seem to be more lucky.

I really sucked at driving. My first five races ended with me being towed off the track. I would overdrive, loop the car, accidentally run into other cars, hit the wall, or wind up in the catch-fence. If you had seen me drive then, you would have told me to find a different hobby. It was a renewed challenge to learn how to drive a race car, how to fix things, how to read track conditions, and how to set up a car. In business, I learned that if you want to speed up your learning curve, ask questions. Lots of them. And like in business, if you want to grow, you need to focus on what you are doing, not on what others are doing. It's hard to steer a car or a business if all your time is spent looking at who or what is beside you.

The best drivers usually have really good down-the-track vision. If you find yourself getting into a lot of wrecks, it's because you are looking at the bumper of the car in front of you, so when something does happen, you don't have enough time to react. Those who look way down the track seem to be able to stay out of more wrecks. You can't win if you don't finish, and you can't finish if you are in a lot of wrecks. Just like in business, the further you can look ahead, the better. It gives you more time to plan and adjust.

You don't have to win to be a winner. If you do better than you expected, that can be more rewarding than winning. What I mean is, I sucked at racing, but as I was learning, I slowly got better. My expectations were relatively low. Just finishing a race was a goal. I would be ecstatic to finish. Then I started getting top 10s, then top 5s, and then eventually got lucky and won a race. My first win, I was shocked. I had not arrived at the track expecting to win. As the years went by, my wins increased. I was continuing to learn. I was getting better.

Then something happened that changed the way I looked at my racing. I won second in a really big race. I was totally stoked. I wanted to jump on the roof of the car and scream holy shit, I got second. I went to the race just hoping to make the feature event. I had already won by getting to race the feature. There were about 80 cars at the event and only 24 would make the feature. Getting second in the feature was icing on the cake.

I went over to the winner of the race to congratulate him. I shook his hand and said, great job. He didn't seem very happy. I went and congratulated the guy who got third, and he also didn't seem very happy. I thought about it and the next time I saw them, I asked why they didn't seem very happy with their respective results. The winner said, well, I was hoping to lap more of the field than I did. The third-place finisher said he had started on pole and it was his race to win, but he didn't. He felt he should have won. In both cases, their expectations got the best of them.

Turns out winning doesn't give you as much personal satisfaction as doing better than you thought you would. And if you expect to win all the time, you will be disappointed more, even when you do win.

If you have never been to a circle dirt race track, go check it out sometime. You will see competition, community, and passion. You will see a competitor helping another competitor fix his or her car to get back on the track for the next race. You will see someone win that you thought never would. You will see a 14-year-old kid wheel by the local track champion and beat him. You will see a guy win who takes off his helmet and looks like your grandpa who has been racing 50 years, or in some cases, just started racing. You will see disappointment and redemption. You will see a fleet of volunteers helping with everything from track prep to officiating. You will see fans cheering for their favorite drivers, win or not. You will see a pack of loud and powerful race cars going into a corner super fast and somehow all coming out of it without running into each other. Like a choreographed scene, it will amaze you. And yes, sometimes you will see wrecks and chaos, which I'm not a big fan of.

Nascar gets a lot of attention, but if you want to see some exciting racing, go check out your nearest dirt track. It's like a small hometown diner, one where you will find some of the best food on earth. For some, they go once and they are hooked for life. Others don't see much value in it. For me it's entertaining, challenging, and also rewarding. Racing is also where I picked up the nickname the Red-Headed Rebel.

Back to the purpose of the book. The next chapter explains how we utterly failed at getting principles into the culture on our first attempt. We went back to the drawing board and tried again with a very different approach. Persistence paid off, and we got it right on the second try.

Winning King of The Dirt
- Photo courtesy of All The Dirt! Racing News, Inc.

. . .

Qualifying at Mississippi Thunder Speedway - Photo by Phil Haney

Racing action at the Jamestown Speedway - Photo by Cody Papke

Scott racing next to his son in law, Joey Rowell - Photo by Cody Papke

3
CREATING CULTURE

"For individuals, character is destiny.
For organizations, culture is destiny"
—Tony Hsieh

I remember writing a big hairy audacious goal of making $25 million in sales. RealTruck was betting on focusing on creating an outstanding company culture to help get us there. In addition, I set forth an even greater goal of reaching $100 million in sales by 2025. We bet the company could reach this goal mostly due to the company culture we were developing. It was a long bet, but one that paid off. We not only reached the $25 million goal quickly, but we also reached $50 million way before we thought, and reached the $100 million goal, many years before that timeline.

Culture develops with or without guidance. If you want a better outcome, especially in business, I recommend you develop a culture strategy and provide guidance; otherwise, its natural development will lean toward being fear-based, ruthless, competitive, and cutthroat. Culture is everywhere. Sports teams and their fans have it, companies and divisions have it, offices and departments have it. Countries, states, cities, and blocks have it. Families, churches, schools, and classrooms have it. Big and small groups of people have it. It's everywhere.

Culture is defined as the attitudes and behaviors characteristic of a group. Whether the group realizes it or not, decisions and policies are influenced by this Those attitudes and characteristics are driven by the pervasive principles that are adopted by the group, whether formally or informally. This can develop sponta-neously without much thought or attention. It can be plagued with inconsisten-cies in policies and practices because of warped values that vary based on who or what level of status a given person or group of people have in that culture. Like a company that has a policy of no alcohol at company events, except sales reps who do it while golfing with customers because that's different. Or execu-tives who can also drink at a company party, but no one else can.

Many employee handbooks will get your eyes pretty dilated trying to under-stand all the exceptions to the rule, and which employee what does and doesn't apply. They tend to try to police the exception rather than reward the rule. All seem to favor those who have authority, because for their more important work, they require company policies be more flexible for the sake of good business practice. These attitudes drive the behavior; therefore, the right principles need to be in place in order to encourage the behaviors desired by a company. If you want to create a family-friendly culture, you need to have principles in place that support this. Then you can evolve to having things such as day care, flexible work hours, and family activities like picnics. These benefits let everyone work-ing within and outside the company know that family is a strong value everyone shares within the workplace. However, if you don't have a core value or guiding principle embedded into the company culture around family, then you may see those benefits, but there will be many exceptions and inconsistencies around them. Profit motive, managing the exception, and fear will make their way into company policy and attitudes.

If you can get the principles right, the right attitudes are created and the right behaviors will follow. A company culture will spontaneously occur and evolve over time, moving in the direction those principles encourage. If you don't have core values or guiding principles, those behaviors and attitudes will evolve over time towards each individual's interpretation of coworker and com-pany ideas, attitudes, and actions. You can either stand by and hope a positive culture will develop with positive principles on its own, or you can purposefully create and nourish the culture.

Years ago, the New Orleans Saints[6] were caught with the bounty scandal or #bountygate. It had become totally acceptable for coaches to encourage their players to hurt players from other teams—and was even incentivized with praise and financial bonuses. They had created an internal culture that made this attitude and subsequent behavior acceptable, and they encouraged it. It was amplified with social, emotional, and financial incentives. All just part of the job.

Once word got out that The Saints were doing this, social shame took over. No one blamed it on culture, but that's what it was. Clearly, winning at any cost was a principle the team was operating on; that developed attitudes that were accepted by the organization, and then the behavior of those attitudes followed. Fortunately, there were heavy sanctions placed upon the team, its managers, players, and coaches. A year later the sanctions were lifted because the NFL Commissioner determined the fault was not with the players, but with the coaches who created and promoted this destructive culture. So, it's just good business to make sure the principles or core values a company lives by are in line with the mission and objectives of the company.

Normally, most company mission statements are pretty good. But if the incentives are not aligned and the principles a company lives by not clearly defined, then you are sure to have some wild west policies and practices take place. And there may be little scrutiny from employees who may not speak up if you don't have a value around open and honest communication because the fear of losing their job will be greater than doing the right thing.

When RealTruck was only a couple years old, there was an incident with a customer service rep. He put a customer on hold, turned, and told me a shipping carrier had run over the package and he didn't know what he should tell the customer. In hindsight, he was really asking me to set the direction for handling such calls. To me, the answer was obvious. Tell the customer what really happened. "We are very sorry about this. We are making arrangements to ship out another package; we will expedite it, and please let us know if there is anything else we can do to make this right."

---

6   Source: *The New Year Times*—search New Orleans Saints bounty scandal

CHAPTER 3

The rep was looking to me for guidance, and my decision would set the stage for other similar interactions with clients. Would he have lied if I told him to? He must have his own principles he lives by, his own set of values, but at work, he may be willing to flex them based on what he sees and is told, because he may fear that if he goes against the establishment it could cost him his job. At that time our culture wasn't clear and our principles were not established, and therefore every decision employees made was based on their perception, accurate or not, of what they felt I would do or what I would think was best for the company. Ours was an unofficial series of perceived rules and sometimes written policies stacked on top of each other for handling situations as they came up. This makes for a lot of inconsistencies in how employees, partners, and customers are treated.

For example, at one time, the TSA had a policy[7] that, in order to take a beverage through security, you would have the traveler take a drink of it. Seems like a good policy. Well, its execution was all over the board. Mothers with breast milk would be told they had to take a drink of it or throw it away by some TSA agents. Other agents saw the flaw in the policy and found workarounds. If you were a mother traveling with a bottle of breast milk, you never knew what you were gonna get. This is where having guiding principles can help. Guiding principles can prevent issues like this from happening, or bring issues like this to the surface quickly and find faster solutions for them. Clearly, the TSA's principles need to be around security, passenger safety, accuracy, and communication, and those principles might be way different than what you might find at a company like RealTruck, which has a very different mission.

At that same time, I had a friend who was a sales rep for a big pharmaceutical company. The laws and policies had changed where reps couldn't "wine and dine" or take doctors on trips anymore. It became harder to book enough time with a doctor to educate them about a specific medication. It was common practice to "fix" your call report showing you were calling on and seeing way more doctors than what the rep was actually doing. My friend, who is honest

---

7   Source: Google.com—search "TSA Mothers Forced To Drink Breast Milk"

and has high character in his personal life, adopted this practice. The result is that his company received bad data, but he was able to keep his job.

Why were these people willing to lie? If management knew what was going on in the field, they might adjust their techniques to improve getting in front of doctors. But with bad data, they were more likely to continue the same processes that don't work. As for the reps, I'm sure they all look at themselves as good, honest folks. Yet many people in the industry, at the time, became ok with "doctoring" their call reports. Why were they willing to set aside their character and principles at work, when they would not do this in their personal life? Today, I realize this kind of behavior comes from fear and a lack of trust within the culture.

In 2010, I was waiting for a flight from Las Vegas after attending the SEMA show. I had begun attending the show in 1993 when I was working for a pickup accessories manufacturer. I reflected on my disappointment in this year's conference as we awaited our flight home. The show seemed to be focused on the pursuit of "more." More sales, more employees, more vendors, more products, more, more, more.

Jeff Vanlaningham, our company president, gave me a copy of the book Delivering Happiness by Tony Hsieh. It was a book about company culture. I was very grateful for the gift, not realizing it would become the second spark for RealTruck's renewed game-changing adventure.

HOW TO FAIL AT CREATING CULTURE

"Failure is simply the opportunity to begin again, this time more intelligently."
—Henry Ford

A few years earlier, in 2008, we had attempted to improve our company culture. We had grown into a multi-million dollar company, but for me, it was becoming hard to go into work. It seemed like, while every direction of the company was pushing forward full steam, I had lost the knowledge of why we were pushing so hard. RealTruck's function as a company was that it had become an easy place to buy truck accessories online, and I was becoming rich because of it. Growing up a poor kid, I had always wanted to have some money, but getting rich because RealTruck was a place to buy truck accessories online didn't seem very fulfilling.

Getting rich wasn't my true purpose, and I felt a bit empty inside. I looked at profit like the blood in the human body. It was required for life, but it did not give the body a purpose, a reason to exist. What was RealTruck's purpose? Why did RealTruck exist, beyond selling truck parts? What should it be? Jeff Vanlaningham had been asking me, "What makes RealTruck unique? What's different with RealTruck compared to everyone else who sells pickup accessories online? What's RealTruck's purpose? Why does RealTruck exist?" That prompted me to ask myself, why did I exist? I reflected on our younger college days and my earlier goal of wanting to be useful above all else.

I couldn't give him a clear answer on why RealTruck existed. It seemed a good time to figure out RealTruck's purpose besides just selling pickup accessories. That in itself was clearly not enough for me and probably the people I worked with. Don't get me wrong; up to this point as a company had accomplished some amazing things- selling $1, $2, $4, $6, and then $8 million online, moving into bigger facilities, winning an innovation award, and more. Certainly we couldn't have foreseen the success we had up to this point. Day after day, year after year, it just happened. There was a time a company flew in on a jet to see RealTruck and offered to buy us. We were developing some really cool tools on the website. But why? For the sake of making money didn't hold enough depth for me. I racked my brain on why RealTruck existed.

Jeff helped transform RealTruck from being a pickup accessories company that sells online to an e-commerce company that happens to sell pickup accessories. He taught us that if we want to be good at e-commerce, we shouldn't be following companies in our industry; rather we should follow companies that were good at e-commerce. Jeff gave me a list of e-commerce companies to watch and called out Zappos.com as being one to look at closely. They were on their way to selling a billion dollars worth of shoes online, had a crazy fun work environment, and they weren't the cheapest place to buy shoes. That intrigued me. But they were started with money and clearly were run by a genius, who sold his last company for $240 million and who had gone to an Ivy League school. They came out of Silicon Valley and had lots of smart people who were very talented. We were just some good ol' hard-working North Dakota folks who learned as we went. Jamestown has about 16,000 people. There weren't too many folks willing to relocate there. Over time, when people asked where we were from, I learned to say Jamestown, ND, 90 miles west of Fargo. That was quicker than saying Jamestown, ND, and then having them ask, where's that?

Even though I felt they were out of our league, we started learning everything about Zappos and discovered they had core values that they practiced at work. Pondering everything I was learning, it struck me what I wanted RealTruck's mission to be: to make people's lives and vehicles better. I pitched the idea to Jeff and Justin Deltener. They looked at me funny. They conceded that some of the more useful products we sold did make people's vehicles better, but how could a company also really make people's lives better? I didn't know, but I did know we had the right people in place to give it a try.

We kicked out our new mission to the entire company. I could sense their reluctance to embrace it, but I figured no one thought RealTruck was a good idea when we started and this would be no different.

Jeff and I then crafted RealTruck's core values.

- Be Helpful First

- Be Fun and Productive

- Continue To Grow

- Unity with Individuality

Each core value had a paragraph explaining the value. We then had them printed, hung them on the walls, got a copy on everyone's desk. And spent the next 18 months wondering why no one was embracing them.

REALTRUCK'S ORIGINAL CORE VALUES

BE HELPFUL FIRST

Helping others is the cornerstone of any successful business or personal philosophy. RealTruck strives to implement this on a daily basis. Whether offering help to our customers or to each other, we go the extra mile to ensure success. In this changing economy, it is important that we stand out from our competitors, and we do this by providing outstanding service by keeping this value at the forefront of our efforts. It has been said that the bottom line is all that matters, but in reality, the core of all that we do as people, whether at work or in our personal lives, is our willingness to help and be helped. It is part of the fabric of our society and it greatly affects the bottom line. A helpful attitude and spirit will make the difference between thriving or just barely making it.

BE FUN AND PRODUCTIVE

These two don't have to be a mutually exclusive deal. In fact, when done right, they complement each other quite nicely. We want RealTruck to be an enjoyable experience for the people who shop with us, the people who we do business with, and the people who work here. If you enjoy what you are doing, it will show. Our office features a strict "no tie" policy that has never been violated. We also are looking forward to the Annual RealTruck Olympics, featuring such prestigious events as the chair twirling contest and the paper airplane flight contest. Have fun, smile and be productive are not just "cutesy clichés" but actually principles we implement every day.

CONTINUE TO GROW

We are not talking about
the bottom line sense of growth
(although that would be nice,
too). We realize that everything
changes. What works today might
not work tomorrow. Is there
a way this can be done better?
We welcome feedback from our
customers, suppliers and our staff.
Each suggestion is an opportunity
to improve how we work and
how we live. The greatest barrier
to growth is closed-mindedness,
and we refuse to let what we think
we know stand in the way of our
development.

Original Core Values flier

UNITY WITH INDIVIDUALITY

A company is nothing more than the sum of the people that make it work.
These people, being united in direction and purpose, can do much more than
just contribute to the bottom line. Their dedication, passion, and uniqueness
enrich the lives of everyone around them. These diversified personalities all
work toward a common goal while having an enduring respect for each other's
distinct qualities. This respect makes a job a career and a career more like just
having fun.

As you can see, Jeff and I did a fairly decent job writing them. They are
good values most would want to have. But in getting them into the culture, we
failed utterly.

BACK TO THE WHITEBOARD

I was shocked that no one was embracing our new core values. I thought, *You are empowered with these values- go and do great things to support our mission of making people's lives and vehicles better.*

Eighteen months into our failed experiment, most folks didn't know what the values were, even though they were plastered everywhere. I was utterly discouraged. But fortunately, we did not allow this to be the end of the story. One of the lessons I learned along the way is that sometimes if an idea fails, many times, it pays to repackage it and try again.

Back to the book Jeff gave me at the beginning of the chapter. While returning from SEMA Las Vegas in 2010, I noticed that Jeff and I weren't sitting together. It was a one-stop flight followed by a 90-minute drive home. Normally, when we travel together we can talk for hours on end. However, this trip, sitting by myself, I began reading the Delivering Happiness book. I was amazed, inspired, and couldn't put it down. I read it non-stop all the way home.

Tony, the author of Delivering Happiness, created a billion-dollar company and he bet it all on culture. He believed that if they could get the culture right, everything else would come into place. And he was right.

Why couldn't we do this right here in North Dakota at RealTruck? Zappos doesn't have anything that RealTruck couldn't have. Yes, they started with some money; yes, they had a great leader. But Tony bet it on culture. Tony also had the experience of creating a company that he lost passion for and sold it. At Zappos, he didn't want to go down the same path as his first company. I didn't want to sell RealTruck and start over. Could we try again? Could we double down and get the culture going in the right direction? What would it take? I wanted RealTruck to be useful and I wanted RealTruck to make people's lives better. We had failed at our first attempt to instill core values into the company. I thought that if we did some of the things Zappos does, we also could have a higher purpose. One that makes people's lives better, that is rewarding to those who work at RealTruck and those who do business with RealTruck.

Becoming rich was not fulfilling. Selling more pickup accessories for the sake of selling more was not fulfilling. Making RealTruck better for our employees, staff, and partners, now that was an attractive thought. Could we be an example or even an icon for how a company should treat customers, staff, and partners? Could we do it right here in North Dakota? That seemed like an impossible goal given we tried once and utterly failed before. So I slept on it.

ON FIRE — CULTURE 2.0

I woke up the next morning totally on fire. But it was a cautious and controlled flame, deep within my inner being. What did we have to lose? Nothing. What did we have to gain? Everything. Tony and Zappos did it. Why couldn't we?

I did some Internet searching and found what I thought were the books that influenced Tony and Zappos. I ordered Good to Great, Tribal Leadership, and How Great Companies Get Their Mojo. I went on a book reading binge of all binges. I read those books and more. Anything I could find on making

My first of many Delivering Happiness *books*

us better. I ordered those three books along with Delivering Happiness for Jeff and Justin. I insisted they read them, even while they were at work. Those four books became the pillars for what we were about to create. They would be the books I would give to anyone working at RealTruck and anyone wanting to make their business better. If you enter my office today, you will notice multiple copies of my favorite business books which I encourage employees to take and read.

They say hindsight is 20/20. Now I can see what went wrong with our first attempt and what went right with our second.

WHY COMPANIES FAIL AT CULTURE

Here is a list of reasons why companies try and ultimately fail at establishing a winning culture. When referring to core values, principles, and guiding principles, I mean the same thing.

1. Fail to get input from everyone at the company.
2. Put them on the wall before they are practiced and understood by the employees.
3. Fail to show how people's personal values tie into and align with the company's values.
4. Don't reward, recognize, hire or fire by their company's values.
5. Skill first rather than character and culture fit first hiring policy.
6. Fail to call out examples of practicing the company's guiding principles.
7. They have good ideas, but not the freedom to take risks, which means they're bad at executing ideas or even attempting to.
8. Fail to encourage and provide resources for employees and managers to have gatherings to ask questions on how they can practice their values better.
9. Fail to be transparent with what they are doing as a company. When leadership isn't open and transparent, neither are the troops. It's hard to work as a team or unit if everyone has their own private agenda.

10. Fail at helping each and every employee see how what they do fits into the bigger picture, mission, and objectives of the company.

11. Don't base decisions on values and principles first, but rather let profit motive trump any principle anytime.

12. Have policies that are in conflict with a principle the company has, with no desire to change the policy.

13. Don't use principles to question why they do what they do or don't do.

14. Have a top-down mentality. Nothing in the values empower employees to question management or policies.

15. Don't spend enough time or resources learning how to practice principles.

16. Let *profit-motive* overrule a *principle or value* repeatedly. This one is listed twice because it's the biggest offender of a bad culture.

GUIDING PRINCIPLES 2.0 ROLLOUT PROCESS

> **❝***If you don't see what you want to be,*
> *be what you want to see.*
> *If you don't hear want you want to hear,*
> *say what you want to hear.***❞**
> —*Peggy Martin*

I was inspired again and on fire with purpose. It is difficult to maintain that level of excitement, so I needed to act quickly. We decided we were going to bet the farm on the idea that if we could get the culture right at RealTruck, everything else would fall into place. Jeff and Justin were onboard.

My first action was to email the entire company and ask them what their personal values were. What are the principles they live by or try to live by? What are the values they have or aspire to have? If we were to be successful, it was important that everyone in the company could see how their personal principles (values) lined up with the company's principles. I also asked everyone to write a list of things they were grateful for and to share that with me and others. As the answers came back, I began creating a list. As I looked at it, it made me smile. It was clear folks valued learning, growing, and wanting to be helpful. All really good values. Even if they were worded slightly differently, we grouped like values. Then we came up with quick, to-the-point names for each of the groups.

Below are some of the real examples and the guiding principles they were in sync with:

DELIVER MORE

"Treat everyone the way you'd want to be treated by them if they were in your shoes."

"Don't ever let someone feel they are being taken for granted."

"Leave it better than you found it."

"Do the best I can and always try my hardest."

"Don't be a jackass (be considerate)."

"Anything worth doing is worth doing right the first time."

"Be helpful to others." Next level: "Be helpful to others and remain anonymous."

"Be nice to everyone I meet."

"Be helpful whenever I can. It makes me feel good and seems to be the right thing to do."

"Don't ever let someone feel taken for granted."

"Give love, kindness, tolerance rather than demand them."

"Having strong patience."

"Help others and expecting nothing in return."

"Help people."

"Do things even if it is inconvenient."

"Love."

"Share a friendly smile, welcoming that person or spreading the gift of love, as love has many meanings."

"Be a good friend."

"Be helpful when someone needs help."

"Work hard."

"With patience and determination you will eventually succeed and be greatly rewarded."

TRANSPARENCY ROCKS

"Be a good listener."

"Shut up and don't judge."

"Be understanding because we are all human with lessons to be learned from experiences and mistakes."

"Tough love means telling the truth when you know it needs to be told."

"Always look for my mistakes in any situation."

"Patience."

"Be open to truthful criticism."

"Be a good communicator."

"Be open with more people."

"I want people to know the real me more."

"Be honest with people… trust is really hard to earn back once you've shown people you are not honest."

"Be understanding."

"Be respectable."

"Be real."

IMPROVE

"Continue to learn new things so I can be a better me."

"Never stop learning."

"There is always more to learn and it can help make you a better person."

"Always keep an open mind and be willing to listen and learn. As much as you think you know, you can always grow from the people around you."

"Ask myself what opinion or belief could I be wrong about today."

"Continue to be a spiritual seeker/spiritual apprentice."

"There is always more to learn and it can help make you a better person."

"Stay strong even when times get tough."

"Stay open-minded."

"Be a better me."

"Focus on the big picture and don't get caught up in tunnel vision."

"Grow in helpfulness and understanding."

"Leave it better than you found it."

"Be happy most of the time."

"Be happy: start each day new and fresh."

Things relating to being happy we placed here. They could also go under Be Humble. The reason they were placed under Improve is because learning and improving are strong ways to increase one's happiness baseline.

"Leave what you cannot change in the past and move forward."

"Try to learn from everyone…every man is my teacher….some teach what I want to be and others teach what I don't want to be."

"Be the best I can be."

"Be the best grandma and mother and mother-in-law I can be."

"Try to be a positive example, or more specifically not be a negative example."

"Try to be a patient learner."

TAKE RISKS

"Be understanding because we are all human with lessons to be learned from experiences and mistakes."

"Don't be afraid to try new things."

"You may fail, but there is value in the attempt even if the result is not what you had hoped, or you might find a new loved talent or activity."

"Do some amazing things."

"Be determined because sometimes hanging in there a little longer is the
difference in success or failure."

"Dedication. Staying on course in a situation and never giving up."

"Don't be afraid to try new things."

"Try new things."

"Take more calculated risks."

"Be willing to try more things."

"Realize failure is part of being successful."

INCLUDE FUN

"Laugh at yourself; everyone else is."

"Be happy most of the time."

"Have fun."

"Not take myself so seriously."

"Be more funny."

"Laugh more."

"Have a good time with whatever I am doing."

"Partake in more fun activities."

"Make more time to have fun."

"Try to have fun at everything I do."

"Try more fun things."

"Smile more than I do."

"Experience joy and happiness more often."

BE HUMBLE

"Give back and give forward. Giving back because lots of people have
helped me along the way, and giving forward because a good leader
helps others be even more successful down the road."

"Help others be even more successful down the road."

"Giving back."

"Eliminate the phrase 'that's not my job' from your vocabulary."

"Catch others doing things right."

"Always find the good in any situation and find the best of everyone."

"Always look for my mistakes in any situation."

"Not be mean when I'm having a bad day."

"Appreciation. Taking just a couple seconds out of the day to say thank you
to a deserving someone."

"Are people under-achieving or am I over-expecting?"

"Be a good sport…Win or lose.."

"Lead others by example and try to follow the most moral path."

"Say please and thank you."

"Treat everyone around you very well."

Some of the statements we received were, "Always keep an open mind and be willing to listen and learn," and "As much as you think you know, you can always grow from the people around you." These statements could qualify as principles under a variety of groups: Transparency Rocks, Improve, Take Risks, and Be Humble.

Jeff and I were both marketers. We decided to roll them out as Guiding Principles rather than core values. We hoped the principles would guide how we made decisions, worked, and played together. We wanted them to guide our actions with everything we did at RealTruck. Of course, we needed to learn to do this as we went along. We were not seeking perfection, but rather progress. Moving more and more in the direction of principles first. It was decided early on, we did not want to put the new guiding principles on the wall the first year. We wanted to get better at practicing them. After we grouped everyone's personal values and principles into six buckets, we gave them master group names.

We developed a paragraph that describes each principle in more detail. This took a little time as Jeff, Justin, and I debated passionately about how the long descriptions for each principle were exactly worded. I think we somehow knew the long descriptions might be hard to change down the road. We rolled out one principle at a time. Each time we released a principle, the announcement ended

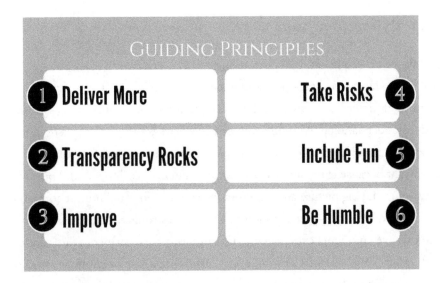

with this: "If you have this principle, or wish to have it, then RealTruck will be a great place to grow and work. We will hire, reward, and recognize people by this. If you do not have or aspire to have this principle, then RealTruck will not be a good experience for you."

Our Mission is simple—to make people's lives and vehicles better. We do this by practicing our guiding principles. These are the fundamentals we strive to live and work by.

DELIVER MORE

Delivering more than expected is our first guiding principle. The "status quo" is never enough. We have a duty to go above and beyond what is expected, to fulfill unrecognized needs, create surprise and serendipity leading to a lasting emotional impact and connection. Delivering more creates smiles and memorable experiences. To be exceptional, we must constantly deliver more and find creative ways to do this with our customers, coworkers, and partners. We must be determined to do this to an ever-increasing degree. A helpful spirit and highly considerate actions are the essential requirements to deliver more.

TRANSPARENCY ROCKS

We value strong and lasting relationships. It is critical for relationship-building to have effective, open, and honest communication. Communication is always difficult in any organization, being transparent eliminates guesswork and misunderstanding. We want everyone to always try to go to any length to encourage transparent, thorough, complete, and effective communication. It is important because everyone needs to understand how each of us and our teams connect to the big picture and what our mission is. Clear and honest communication, guided by transparency allows us to create stronger, lasting relationships and positive emotional experiences with our customers, partners, teams and each other. Work takes on new meaning, instead of a task or chore; we are now doing something for a friend. We are able to transmit a genuine attitude of caring that translates into service made visible.

IMPROVE

With an open mind and a passionate spirit, pursue innovation and ongoing improvement. Let's wrap our hearts and minds around the idea of ongoing change. Create it, drive it, embrace it, inspire it and lead it. Status quo is the curse of business and we want to be extraordinary. Constant change is something we seek. Not only do we seek change, we want to be the creators of it. Companies can copy our policies and ideas, but they can't copy our people or our spirit. Innovation must come from everywhere in our company. Find ways to do more with less and remember "good enough" is the enemy of the great. Each of us need to spend time learning new things personally and professional for ongoing improvement. Working hard and putting in the extra effort is what creates great transformation. We should be adventurous and always be striving to make something better.

TAKE RISKS

Don't be afraid to take risks. Leadership doesn't come from authority, rather the ability to help others achieve more than they thought they could. You have the authority and power to take risks and make mistakes. It is ok to make mistakes, provided we learn from them. Don't accept status quo or that's how we've always done it. We should be adventurous and always be striving to make something better. We want to be creative and unconventional with our solutions. An entrepreneurial spirit and taking risks is needed and is what allows us the possibility of being exceptional.

INCLUDE FUN

Don't just have fun, create it. We want RealTruck to be an enjoyable and memorable experience for our customers, partners and each other. In our pursuit of happiness, we want to add fun and excitement to all areas of our company. From how we design our web pages, conduct meetings to our interaction with people, we strive to practice our guiding principles. We believe the happier and more enjoyable we are the more productive we can be. Always remembering, that we take our responsibilities serious, but not ourselves.

BE HUMBLE

We must be respectful of everyone and treat everyone just like we would want to be treated if we were in their position. There can't be anything that needs to be done that is beneath me. Our successes are important, but we must not let that go to our head. We should not praise ourselves, but rather let our customers, partners, and coworkers do it for us. An ethic of giving back and forward is highly valued. Being grateful for what we have, not taking anything for granted, being of service, helping others reach their fullest potential, setting up others for future success and making the future better is the spirit of being humble. When praised, we should give thanks and pass on credit. When we fall short, we should accept responsibility by being willing to correct and learn from it.

Those six principles would change and propel RealTruck into a company with a greater purpose and passion than I could have ever imagined. Evangelistic customers, employees, and partners. There were loads of fun, innovation galore, and a spirit of commitment and teamwork most would come to love. It was always a work in progress. We were not perfect. We would go on to change the game in the pickup accessories world. It was humbling.

. . .

Jeff Vanlaningham & Justin Deltener on Sweater Day

Team visit to Google campus

4

DELIVER MORE

"The status quo sucks."
—George Carlin

"Status quo, you know, is Latin for 'the mess we're in.'"
—Ronald Reagan

Delivering more than expected is our first guiding principle. The "status quo" is never enough. We have a duty to go above and beyond what is expected, to fulfill unrecognized needs, create surprise and serendipity leading to a lasting emotional impact and connection. Delivering more creates smiles and memorable experiences. To be exceptional, we must constantly deliver more and find creative ways to do this with our customers, coworkers, and partners. We must be determined to do this to an ever increasing degree. A helpful spirit and highly considerate actions are the essential requirements to deliver more.

1. Deliver More

We analyzed again what went wrong the first time we tried to establish core values for the company. Our next step was to present our new set of guiding principles for everyone to get to know and implement. We felt re-branding them all as guiding principles would help all of us have the awareness these were the principles to guide us in our ideas, attitudes, and actions.

We decided for the rollout that we would focus on one guiding principle at a time for two months before moving on to the next. I was adamant that they not be on the wall to read, but in our hearts and minds to do. Even after we got all the principles into the culture, we tended to repeat this process of really focusing on one for a couple of months.

Once we felt we were practicing a given principle reasonably effectively, we would put a poster-size graphic around the offices. We sent out an email to the company explaining our plan, to introduce them to our new guiding principles. I followed this with a quick ten-minute video, as I had discovered video was a great, fast way to share something with the entire company, especially one that is spread over multiple locations. I ended both the email and the video with this:

> *These are the principles RealTruck wants to work and play by. If you have them or want to have them, RealTruck will be a great place for you to work and grow. We will try to practice them in everything we do, from hiring and firing to rewarding and recognizing. If you don't have them or want to have them, then RealTruck will not be a good place for you to work and grow.*

We began the process of merging personal values with work values. Refer back to Chapter 3 for a refresher on how we did this. We found that people often have great personal values but can struggle with putting them to practice in everyday work situations. Our hope was that if we could shape our work culture to empower people's great personal values, then anything is possible.

Delivering more encompasses customers, employees, and partners. Our partners were other B2B businesses we worked with, such as our suppliers, banks, outside accountants, landlords and shipping carriers like UPS.

With each guiding principle, we asked all the managers, supervisors, and teams to get together and talk, ask questions, and get answers.

QUESTIONS WE NEEDED ANSWERS TO

We needed to know what to do more of and what we needed to do less of, along with understanding what was standing in our way. Here are the questions we started with:

1. What can we do to deliver more to our customers?
2. What can we do to deliver more to our partners?
3. What can we do to deliver more to each other?
4. What things are we doing that are not even at status quo?
5. What things are standing in the way of us delivering more?
6. What is stopping me from delivering more?

This is the original email and combined list that was given to everyone in the company:

> *Hi RT Crew,*
>
> *Below is a list of all of the feedback regarding how we can better Deliver More. Answers are combined generally when possible. There is a great deal of information here and we have a lot of ideas. Some mission and vision clarification could help better refine the list as there are some ideas that conflict with others. (I.e. discount more versus just focus on good prices). This is a great start.*

Below is the combined list from all departments of the feedback we received. In the spirit of Transparency Rocks, all of it was shared with the entire company.

WHAT CAN WE DO TO DELIVER MORE TO OUR CUSTOMERS?
*   Free upgrade shipping
*   Send a T-shirt just because
*   Return-customer gifts

- Special return-customer discounts (Come-back discount)
- Sending customer b-day cards
- Questionnaire to customers asking what they want instead of guessing
- Customer showcase (customers share pics, experiences, etc.)
- For my vehicle (if customer creates account, special link to what fits their vehicle)
- Full vehicle info center (supply info about their vehicle, spec sheets, etc.)
- Help Desk (customer can ask a question through a help desk system which ties into the customer's account)
- Loyalty program
- Mid-experience survey
- Overall philosophy of Open and Honest
- Robust online account
- Wow our customers with service
- Treat everyone with respect and courtesy (customers, vendors, employees)
- Review restocking fees
- Evaluate pricing
- Employ a Spanish-speaking service rep
- Provide all the useful information a customer could need
- Expand social interaction (perhaps including a forum on site)
- More videos
- Get the customer excited when they open their order
- Only sell products we believe in
- Remember that even if they don't buy during their visit/call, "we should always send them good vibes."
- Review return history and drop lines with lots of returns, then drop that fee. It will hurt short term, but keep customers long term.
- Instead of concentrating on the "best" price, let's have a "good" price as we can't always beat the best price from Amazon or some of the other super-discounters. Then do two things: concentrate on customer service for repeat business and have lots of sales.
- Aggressively get a Spanish speaker on the phone. I remember hearing "No hablo español" multiple times from the phone pit one day, I'm sure it was a fluke, but still. (Heck, buy a copy of Rosetta Stone for the office—it would be a well-spent $500 if one of our reps used it and learned the language.)
- Provide information that goes above and beyond what we consider the

norm for our industry to our customers in an easy-to-digest form. Our product pages are full of information about accessories, but I think that creating a community for people to express their opinion is what we need to do to take it a step further.

- Having a review system is a step in the right direction. Enhancing our social networks, like Facebook, the blog, and Twitter, are going to be challenging, but should be a priority.
- Video is the wave of the future. People are saying, "Don't tell me, SHOW ME!" Or… "If you do tell me, MAKE IT BRIEF."
- Another way to deliver more is to create a sense of disbelief when a customer receives their product.
- This was WONDERFUL! We rocked his world with fast delivery (I'm assuming free shipping). I want that to happen EVERY TIME! How do we ensure this? Do we have a free gift in every box? When they open the box are they surprised because, "Hey! Wow! A free shirt is in here!"
- We need to become the go-to place not just for truck accessory purchases, but for opinions and community support as well.
- When people think of aftermarket parts and how they want to upgrade their new ride, etc., I want them to think RealTruck. If they want to talk about their tonneau cover with other people, I want them to think of us. If they want to read a review, etc., I want us to come first. Not only in SEO searching, but in general.
- I want us to be REAL! If we are REALTruck, I think we should live up to the name. If we don't particularly think a product we sell is top-of-the-line or of superior grade, we should say so.
- Have website show ESD one day longer (customer will receive tracking one day before they expect it). Under promise and over deliver.
- Provide better expectation with more information. Ask, "What would I want to know as a customer in this situation?" and relay relevant information to customers.
- Do what we say we will do, when we say we will do it
- Be helpful first (what can we do, not what we can't do)
- More accurate information regarding ship times
- Live inventory
- Where to put discount codes in new cart—hard to find for some
- Exclusions/Exemptions from discount codes viewed as scam. Not enough language to call out exceptions at every level.

- Random shipping upgrades
- Random freebee – tonneau tonic with cover
- Phone messages – funnier and/or more personal
- Automate FedEx third party tracking
- Examine all vendors we get tracking from invoices on and eliminate by changing to our accounts
- Shipping insurance should be eliminated
- Ship damage claims – get the replacements moving faster
- The team specifically talked about communicating
- More caring and personal manner with customers
- Better emails to customers
- Take pride in your work; don't fake it. Every project or product that hits our desk must turn into something to take pride in. When you take the extra few minutes to research a specific part, or take a little longer to do a thorough price comparisons, it's the customer who ultimately wins. Through our resources, we can ensure that the customer gets the right part, the first time, and at a competitive price.
- We must ensure that we are doing high-quality work, not just high quantity. We need to take the time to check our work and make sure it's right the first time. This helps prevent returns and also helps reduce call volume from people who have questions because our products are not described properly.
- Validate our personal relationships with customers (empower anyone to send a card, flowers, etc.)
- Truly educate our customers. We have many unanswered questions for parts- ex., difference between light bulbs. What are round vs. square lights good for. Track, log and display questions Customer Service reps get and their answers for all customers to see regarding that part or product line.
- Allow customers to ask questions specifically about the product they are looking at. Email, post a form, or chat about it.
- Answer the phones no matter what. Make it our mantra: we always answer the phones.
- Always respond to questions, emails, and needs in a timely manner
- Do what we say we are going to do
- Better answer and address customer needs

WHAT CAN WE DO TO DELIVER MORE TO OUR PARTNERS?

- Call all vendors regularly
- Ask vendors what we can do for them
- Provide regular customer feedback to vendors
- Is there a way we can come up with a structured format of providing this information? A quarterly blast that goes to each vendor breaking down their star rating, any comments received?
- Treat them all with the same amount of respect
- Start an annual get together that RealTruck hosts to show them how important they are to us
- Split up vendors for OFS to be responsible for a group of vendors
- One point of contact for each vendor
- Automated order confirmations
- Be polite
- Look for and advocate improvements that provide benefits for Customer, RT, and vendors
- Communication
- Updated Vendor information in VE
- Visit vendor facilities
- We must remember that the vendors are our partners and not simply bill collectors
- EDI capability to speed things up and cut down on the paper flow
- Communicate with each vendor on a professional, yet friendly level
- Make vendors want to communicate with us by knowing that we will always be eager to hear from them
- Make sure that when we do need to contact them, we have made an honest effort to answer/resolve any questions before bothering them. By not being the annoying company that always calls for simple things that could have been figured out, they know we are professionals and good partners.
- As a whole, RealTruck can define ownership of certain actions that can prevent sending excessive communication to the vendors as well. We have to contact our vendors on many issues, so we certainly do not want to ask them the same questions more than once.
- Making sure we get the right price on the PO
- Are we asking them what we can improve on?

- Call them more
- Always acknowledge and reply to emails in a timely manner
- Share sales and return data
- Share product feedback so they can be aware of what customers think

What Can We Do To Deliver More To Each Other?

- Learn more about each other
- Understand more about the vision
- Explore/exploit employee talents beyond their job description
- Improve internal communication
- Improve organization and cooperation within the company
- Utilize conferencing software that works well
- Treat each other with respect and dignity
- Make each person on the RealTruck team feel as equally important as the next
- Find hidden talents in each other
- Make a special effort to socialize more
- Let each other know our talents
- Improve internal communication
- Defined areas of responsibility that are known to everyone is one way
- One person that is the "internal knowledge officer" whenever a problem, issue, or idea comes up that you can't resolve yourself—mail the "internal knowledge officer" and it becomes their responsibility to get the info to the right person and follow up.
- Set up weekly training to teach each other stuff (work or personal)
- Pay it forward
- Learn more, earn more program
- Training
- More practical training with products (installation and comparison)
- Breakfasts
- Bingo
- Take vendor incentives as collective for RT employees
- Be aware of what is going on with fellow employees
- No matter what communications/questions come our way from another coworker, we are always ready and willing to help
- Reduce unnecessary workload for our coworkers

- Have IT staff speed up your work machine day
- Offer computer/tech help with home machines
- Assist in setting up home internet security
- Skype training
- How to share photos training
- How to set up a blog, register domain name training
- Video editing training
- Give back to community (adopt a highway, volunteer in a personal/ meaningful way)
- Respond to emails in a timely manner regardless of who sends them. Let each other know when you need it done or when you can have it done. Or if there will be a delay in getting it done.

WHAT THINGS ARE WE DOING THAT ARE NOT EVEN AT STATUS QUO?

- Not updating site fast enough
- Need better, more accurate info on website
- Better discontinued notifications and follow up
- Not batching POs
- Need more accurate ESDs on website
- Not having automate FedEx third party tracking
- Returns
- Ownership/follow-up with customers
- Emails with bad grammar and spelling errors
- Emails not formatted
- Credit memo quo is an impossible task
- Email templates that look nice (internal customer invoice, order status email when we add a note to the customer)
- Several products that are nowhere near optimal health. If we can get to the point where all of our current data is clean, then it is much easier to maintain in the future with just roll-ups and new part additions.
- Catch up to industry standards
- Customer reviews (do it right)
- Better lateral navigation
- Keep shopping button should go to a better page
- Charge with ship instead of authorize and capture right away

- Backorder warnings
- Online chat
- Change policies
- Better tools for returns
- Year, make and model vehicle searching
- Year, make and model display on categories
- More consistent data mapping
- Answering phones
- Resolving vendor issues (many outstanding CMs and ongoing unresolved issues)

WHAT THINGS ARE STANDING IN THE WAY OF US DELIVERING MORE?

- Not being under a common mission
- Ideas of how to deliver more
- Structure and lack of cohesion as a big problem at this point
- With simple projects it's hard to tell who is the lead and who is even involved with the development
- Slow development
- Policy (ship damage)
- Systems (lack of innovation with automation such as tracking, etc.)
- Staffing turnover in customer service
- Sales volumes
- Policies that we have, existing or those that have been created recently, are not being communicated to other departments.
- Not upgrading to a newer version of GP
- Meet with IT but nothing gets started
- Had a meeting with development, but nothing ever came of it
- Manpower
- IT limitations
- Ordering controls
- Image maintenance
- Formal training programs
- Focus and priority
- Say it's great to deliver more, but need to lead by example
- Stakeholders explaining needs, IT understanding needs

WHAT IS STOPPING ME FROM DELIVERING MORE?

- Only me
- Training
- Lack of product knowledge
- General new business acclimation
- Apparent technical issues with video conferencing
- Off-site issues
- Unfamiliarity with staff, their titles and roles
- Time management
- Attitude
- Possibly being apathetic. "We've always done it this way." We need to develop a "thinking out of the box" mentality.
- In some cases we feel that the enhancements we request from IT get put on the back burner and we ultimately are not important
- Time and judgment. It's a challenge to balance work flow with delivering more
- Belief
- Scared to make a mistake
- Not knowing what I can and can't do
- Not knowing if it's OK to change something

This was our starting point. Clearly, everyone had lots of ideas on how we could deliver more and areas needing improvement. There also were conflicts. For instance: Is it delivering more to offer coupon codes? Over time, most of these questions or challenges were resolved by applying our guiding principles to them. The other observation was that departments and people tended to be better at pointing out what another department or person could do to deliver more rather than themselves. We did get better at seeing what we could do to improve internally because of our Transparency Rocks guiding principle.

As mentioned, we asked all the managers to determine from their teams what they needed to do to identify where we are delivering more, where we are failing to deliver more, and where we need to start delivering more to our customers, partners, and each other. The ongoing responses from the front lines was amazing.

We repeated this process every two months over the course of the next year with each guiding principle. And since one of our guiding principles was Take Risks, everyone was empowered to take action and do something that didn't match up to the principles we were going to try to work and play by. The results we started to see were electrifying, uplifting, and just plain wicked cool.

Each week, we had a meeting with all the managers. Initially there were nine of us, so it got the name The 9@9 Meeting. We had up to two minutes to share what was going on in our area. With only two minutes, clearly we had to focus on sharing what was most important. Included in this two minutes, I asked each manager to do a shout-out for someone in their department for delivering more. I would also ask them to do the same thing for someone not in their department. It was important we identify and call out "delivering more" actions outside of our individual departments. It was also important we teach each other what "deliver more" really is with a real example of it.

This meeting would produce the content for a video I would kick out regularly, "What's Up @ RT," and it would include the shout-outs from the managers. The extra bonus in this ongoing practice was a higher level of perceived employee appreciation. When a manager or another employee from one department catches and shouts-out someone not in their own department, practicing a given principle, feeling appreciated, and a better understanding how your actions affect other people throughout various areas of the company is profoundly impactful. Again, I must say how important this was, that folks could see and hear about examples of practicing our principles—to be able to identify them and amplify them.

This practice of shouting-out someone else's success was part of our last guiding principle of Be Humble, which in its long form includes praising others. I also couldn't help but notice that if a manager "forgot" to do this in their previous two minutes, they would definitely include it at the start of the next week. Jeff, Justin, and I would also shout-out at least one of the managers or someone in their department each week as well.

In order to imprint our guiding principles further into the work culture, we turned to merchandising. We made bracelets, buttons, badges, and more with each one of our guiding principles embedded on them. It started when Jeff came up with the idea of creating buttons with "Deliver More" on them. We turned it into a game in which people would try to catch someone personifying one or more of the guiding principles.

Anyone in the company, anytime, could give someone a button when they noticed them delivering more. What started to happen was almost jaw dropping. Gradually, day by day, we started to see lots of people catching lots of people delivering more and giving them a button. Someone else took it a step further and snapped a photo and posted to our private Facebook page along with a note on what they did to get the button.

There were times it brought me to tears. Here you had an entire company of people, all "catching" each other doing things and complimenting them for it. This practice would encompass all of our guiding principles. And of course the marketing team got more and more creative with the buttons. Next thing you know, we had bracelets and pins and so forth. Some people who received them would keep them in their work area, hang them on their cube or around their computer screens. Others would give them to people outside of RealTruck when they saw them practicing one of our principles.

What's Up @ RT Video shared with company

Guiding Principles buttons

Guiding Principle bracelets

One day we had to run into Walmart, and I smiled when I saw the greeter wearing a "Be Humble" bracelet. Another time, at one of our kids' performances, another kid was sporting a "Deliver More" and a "Task Risks" pin on their jacket. Wow.

This practice was one of my favorite activities in the company. In most companies it falls on the leader or manager to do most of the praising, and it can be hard for one person to keep up. By having an entire company all engage in this activity- from the front lines to the board room- it was truly inspirational.

DELIVERING MORE TO EMPLOYEES (EACH OTHER)

Treat your staff very well. That's the right thing to do. If you don't, someone else will.

#HAPPYEMPLOYEES = #HAPPYRESULTS

Even though we wanted to deliver more to customers, partners, and employees, Jeff, Justin, and I felt it was really important that we apply the principle of "Deliver More" to our employees and each other.

To deliver more to employees, we started mailing birthday cards and a $10 bill to the children of the employees of RealTruck. "Wishing you a very Happy Birthday! We hope you have a great day and that all your wishes come true." It was signed by Jeff and me. In order to pull this off we needed the help of marketing, HR, and accounting. It's pretty amazing getting a thank you card or email from an 8-year-old. Getting a gift from someone you didn't expect is really a treat. The added bonus was that it created buy-in to the company's mission from the families of employees.

Over the years, it was like a snowball rolling down a hill. Delivering more just kept growing in ways we could have never imagined. Our efforts created an environment that asked what ways could we deliver more.

Bonnie giving Shane a Deliver More bracelet

Whitney getting a Deliver More button

Tami Olsen about to give some buttons

It was a continued effort to always push the bar a little further. Here are some activities we did:

- We created street signs for everyone with their years of service
- We added a new holiday at Real Truck for each individual employee's birthday. It was a paid day off and their supervisor would also take them out for lunch.
- We created a culture team with folks from various departments who met regularly to discover ways to enhance the culture
- We implemented Quarterly Profit Sharing based on guiding principles rating
- We created a Learn More Earn More Program for Customer Service
- We allowed for employees to help each other in times of need with a Vacation Donation
- Anonymous $50 to those who needed it. A name was submitted, and if approved they would be given $50 anonymously through the company.
- Random Acts Of Kindness Program
- 360 Evaluations
- Annual Compensation Summary Statements
- Exercise room
- Game and relax rooms
- Free pop, coffee, and snacks (within reason)
- Kickass annual parties from gangster themes to murder mysteries
- Job titles like Director of Happiness and Chief People Officer, etc.
- Take Your Kids To Work Day
- Culture funds for departments to use for whatever
- Charity program
- We allowed employees a Christmas gift from three choices.
- RealTruck University
- Library in each office—take a book or give a book to anyone

Card sent to employee's children

- Endless potlucks with endless themes
- Dress-up days from Super Hero and Pajama Day to Don Johnson and Walking Dead
- Bean Counter Award (If someone did something to save the company money, they would get a little parade from accounting and some beans.)
- Annual awards for each guiding principle
- Free RealTruck swag from T-shirts to cups
- New employees got $150 for RealTruck gear
- Employees could purchase products for 10% over our cost
- If you wanted to go to a trade show and had a good business reason, you could go

RealTruck picnic

Rod getting his street sign

Tammy's birthday fun

- Free training on everything from budgeting and digital photography to personal coaching and painting
- Office video battles
- Anonymous random acts of kindness gifts
- Rock-star welcome for new hires
- Farewell parties for those moving on
- Training videos
- Themed fun videos
- Dream space on the wall
- Guiding Principle videos
- If you want to be in a video, just ask
- RealTruck Olympics from chair spinning and paper airplanes to singing and dancing
- Summer picnic
- RealTruck after hours
- Majority of employees would help customer service during Black Friday and Cyber Monday
- RealTruck sports (bowling to softball)
- RealTruck talent contest
- RealTruck town hall
- Manager team-building retreats
- The normal benefits: health insurance, vacation, 3% IRA match, etc.

Some of the company-wide yearly gifts at the end of the year were also a treat to watch folks receive. Like a Zappos gift card so they could experience getting some WOW. One holiday season, employees had the choice between an Xbox, a digital watch, or a shopping spree as their holiday gift. It was interesting to see who picked what. Before we rolled out the guiding principles, one year we bought all of the employees a digital camera. In addition to the camera was training on how to properly use one.

Please do not get the impression that every one of these things were perfectly dialed in and consistently practiced 100% of the time, without exception. First, we are humans, and second is our guiding principles of striving to Improve. No matter what we did, a process was always eligible to be changed,

Gift box from holiday party

Debi got me a signed book from Tony Hsieh

Mary getting some wow from Zappos

Shawn on a movie poster

to evolve to something different, enhanced, trimmed or even in some cases completely stopped.

We created "random actions of kindness" in which each month we would focus on an area, customers, partners, or each other. Our team discovered a father wanted to see his son. The mother had relocated out of state and he hadn't been able to see his son in a few years. The team surprised him with a ticket to go see his kid and volunteered some of their vacation time so he could go see him without worrying financially.

Personal highlights for me, when we hit $25 million and $42.5 million the employees made me a gift box that was pretty badass. Another time, Debi Reberg, our customer service manager, got ahold of Tony Hsieh—one of my business heroes—and talked him into writing a nice note and signing his book for me.

Often we had themed video contests where offices or departments would, for example, do a 4th of July fun video. We would vote on the winner. Themes included the 1970s, holidays, and even a "where are the Michael Jackson Thriller dancers now" video contest.

There were so many things employees did for each other aka coworker serendipity. There was the time we added Shawn Herrick's head to a life size Hangover movie poster on his birthday. Or the countless times one employee left a little sticker on another's computer about how much they appreciated them. One time someone left a note on my pickup window (picture: below, left).

So many great and heart-warming memories. The customer service team provided new shoes for a coworker who was losing weight and had run the soles off his shoes on the treadmill. They bought a winter coat and mittens for another coworker who had just moved to ND and had nothing to prepare her for the cold. They have helped pay for books for someone to attend college, sent

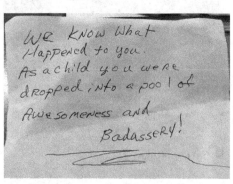

Note left on my car by someone at RT

flowers to our coworkers' loved ones during illness and for funerals, and helped financed getting a bench put in a park for a coworker whose daughter passed. They teamed up and paid to have Auto Start installed on a coworker's vehicle who was raising two small children and had to leave them alone three floors up to run down and start the car to get it warmed up for them in the morning. They helped with a honeymoon stay in a hotel in Denver, gave gas cards to a coworker who lived out of town and was having trouble paying for gas due to some unexpected expenses, paid for a washing machine repair, and even financed a few car repairs along the way.

We took some of the team to San Francisco for training with Delivering Happiness. Much was learned about working as a team. Jeff set it up for us to visit the Google campus, which was no longer open to outsiders, but our fun and transparent relationship with the Google ads team made an exception possible. In addition, we visited the mountains, saw the ocean and the Winchester house, and got to hang out with Chip Conley for an afternoon. Doing things like that meant a lot to everyone. Many of our guiding principles would be enhanced by off-site training or fun activities like this. Please don't get the impression you have to go to California; we did these same kind of team-building activities at the restaurant next door, the local coffee shop, a movie theater, and a fun park.

Delivering Happiness Training in San Fran

DELIVERING MORE TO CUSTOMERS

> ❝ *We see our customers as invited guests to a party,*
> *and we are the hosts. It's our job every day*
> *to make every important aspect*
> *of the customer experience a little bit better."*
> —*Jeff Bezos*

We had a pretty good list to start with. We began to assess what we could do better and where we were falling short. To deliver more to customers, we started sending postcards. The marketing team created some postcards that included fun graphics and themes. These were well received, and customers would often keep them on their fridges at home or their desks at work as some sort of collectible item.

It should be noted that many of our team's activities and strategies can fall into more than one guiding principle. For instance, while we were delivering more to customers through sending postcards, we were also adding an element of fun in our marketing department and for our customers.

In order to show our customers we cared, we made it a priority to ship out new items to replace ones damaged in shipment immediately. Nobody likes to wait. If we really wanted our customers to have the best possible experience with us, we had to make sure our objectives and metrics with our customer service reps aligned with great customer service.

When tracking our metrics, we only measured and reported those things that aligned with great customer service. Customer service rep metrics included time on phone, time available to take calls, and number of serendipity actions, such as postcards and emotional reach-outs. Those were the things they were evaluated on and praised for. Customer serendipity became the internal term for surprising customers with gifts, postcards, phone calls, and other emotionally connecting actions. We dropped phone sales reporting from the metrics for customer service reps. These are metrics for a sales team, and we wanted our customer service reps focused on helping the customer, not selling to them. If we reported individual sales, it would say that sales were important and some would gravitate to trying to sell more, which would conflict with really great customer service if they were rushing a service call to get off the phone in hopes of the next call being a sales call.

We reported company-wide phone sales versus web sales, but not individual sales numbers. We wanted them to help customers find what best fit the individual customer's needs. We didn't want to report on number of calls taken, because if we praised our reps for these numbers, that could lead to reps trying to take as many calls as possible, which in turn would hurt spending the time needed to really help a customer. Measuring their time on the phone and time

Our starter Thank You cards

Fuzzy dice for customers

T-shirts for customers

available to take a call supported a great customer experience along with reporting on benevolent actions like doing personal postcards or mailing out "swag" items to customers, such as free T-shirts and fuzzy dice. We also tried to track and report training time reps took part in.

We wanted customers to have really great experience, but because we were asking questions on how we could deliver more, or asking where we were not delivering more, we started to more quickly recognize areas where we fell short and fix them sooner. We felt if we were delivering more to a customer, a human would always answer the phone first, then transfer them to the next available rep. During really busy business times, we would answer the phone and then put the customer in a call queue for the next available rep. We felt that was better than having the phone call be answered by a machine that puts them in a call queue. We set it up so everyone could see call volumes, and when we needed extra help on the phones, other departments would step up to help.

We also learned it was important to manage expectations. We couldn't be all things to all people. We focused on providing a really great customer experience, period. We decided to build a website that was the easiest place in the world to find accessories that fit a pickup, which is part of a really great customer experience. We stopped offering coupon codes and best price guarantees.

About 40% of the products we offered had some kind of manufacturer's "minimum advertised price" policy or unilateral pricing policy, meaning you couldn't advertise or sell a given product below a certain price. What this means is, if we offered a 10% off sitewide sale, 40% or so of the products couldn't be discounted, which is a real buzzkill and hard for a customer to understand. For coupon codes like this, there would be hundreds of exceptions. So we decided no coupon codes; we would try to price things as competitively as possible without having hoops to jump through. As for most "low price" guarantee policies, or in our case a "best price" guarantee policy, those generally are five to ten-page documents with lots of red and italic writing. We felt this wasn't delivering more to anyone. So we stopped the practice. Both coupon codes and low price policies, for us, fell into the over promise category, which didn't fall in line with a really great customer experience.

We stopped advertising "hassle-free" returns. After all, what return is ever hassle free? Often e-commerce companies try to make it hard for someone to make a return. Restock fees, return shipping, and then having to place a phone call to start a return are three things that piss people off for life. We made an ongoing effort to make returns as easy and painless as possible for the customer. Customers could start a return online or over the phone. We didn't use free returns as a selling point, so customers were often pleasantly surprised when making a return that there would be no restock fee or return shipping cost. We tried to look at them as customers for life, not just one transaction.

Over time, this deliver-more attitude towards customers led to some really neat things.[8] Here are a few of them:

- Free shipping
- Free returns
- No additional handling charges
- Replacement ship damage orders shipped right away
- Always answering phone with real person
- Free swag for customers (dice, T-shirts, stress trucks)
- Customer service team sent personalized postcards to customers (10% was the goal)
- 22% reduction in return rate when we changed to customer service only and no sales reps
- BizRate Platinum Circle of Excellence
- Customer service reps were encouraged to help customers place their own orders online if they didn't know how
- Emails responded to in less than two hours (during business hours)
- No coupon codes
- No "low-price" guarantee policy with five pages of exceptions
- Real product reviews (all product reviews were published)
- Easiest place online to find what fits your truck
- Accurate product recommendations based on your vehicle and geographic area.

---

8   Policies described were how RealTruck operated at the time. They may or may not currently be practiced.

CHAPTER 4

We were definitely killing the status quo and continually asking and searching for new and more effective ways to deliver more.

We spoke to a gal who received some accessories for her husband's truck, as her husband was coming home from deployment, and she mentioned that his truck was his "mistress" and she wanted to "dress her up" for him. She joked about being second place to his truck, and so we sent her a bouquet of flowers saying, "We think the wife deserves a little treat as well," and we included a little USO ornament for their tree.

Another time, a rep discovered a customer had recently lost his wife and was so sad because he wouldn't have a Christmas or anyone to get a present for. The team rallied, learned about the customer, and got him some personalized presents along with a list of places he could get someone a present in need.

We had a customer who called to talk about a tonneau cover, and he mentioned that if he bought it, he would need to send his wife some chocolates, as she would be mad about the amount spent. Debi Reberg, our Director of Happiness, responded that if he bought it, *we* would send her some chocolates, and he laughed and said "OK" as though he didn't really believe us. He purchased, and we sent her a giant box of See's Candies. He wrote a long letter to us, absolutely amazed that we would do this, and as a business owner of a florist and tulip distribution company, sent us some lovely books and said that he was already changing how he does business, based on how we did ours. He was impressed with our being able to be ourselves, our follow-through, and our being able to name ourselves and create our own titles (like "Director of Happiness").

Dee, in customer service, received an upsetting phone call from a customer whose seat covers had not arrived. The woman was extremely upset, more than a missed delivery would warrant. Dee started making conversation with her and realized that the woman was crying. Dee asked her what was wrong, and apparently the woman's daughter had passed away, and they had just buried her a month before. She was raising her grandkids, times were tough, and when she was driving home, she had forgotten and driven past the cemetery (she had been avoiding it) and it made her really upset. We ended up sending her an engraved plaque for her garden, as that is where the daughter spent her final days while she was dying from cancer. Dee and this woman still keep in contact, with occasional phone calls and check-ins.

Alexandra in customer service spoke to a customer who kept checking the backorder of a part because he wanted it in time for Christmas. He stated that it would be his "only Christmas present" because he had just moved and had no family. Alex visited with him quite often on the phone and was able to find out a lot about him. The entire customer service floor purchased gifts for the gentleman, including gloves, scarves, a huge package of North Dakota-made products, a fishing sign for his home, gift cards to restaurants around him, and a bunch of RT swag. We sent a huge box filled with wrapped gifts and made sure it was in time for Christmas. They did this out of their own pockets.

Ed in customer service spoke with a 20+ year Marine veteran who lost his wife and brother in one year, and then suffered a devastating fire which was a total loss of his home and all of his belongings. He made the comment in one of his conversations with Ed that he felt he had no one and nothing left and really missed having a family. Johnny and Ed put together a shadow box (the patches and insignia were removed from Johnny's own uniforms) and they had a custom engraving done saying "You will always have family in North Dakota. Semper Fi."

Over the years, there were so many heart-warming stories. When customers would send an email or write us a card, Debi decided to start putting these on the walls. One wall was filled, then another and another. One day, walking through the office, it struck me.

Customer comments filled wall after wall

I've been buying online since 1998. In that time, I only had one experience that compelled me to write the company and tell them how impressed I was with how well they took care of me. That was Zappos, hand-delivering some shoes to my hotel room in Vegas, when I was at the SEMA show and forgot to pack the proper walking shoes for the show. What amazed me as I stared at the walls around the office was this: Here were notes and letters from thousands of people from around the U.S. who had such a positive experience that they took the time to write us about it. Share with us, with RealTruck, this crazy little company from North Dakota. I was floored and humbled once this realization fully hit me.

DELIVERING MORE TO OUR PARTNERS

*"Love is friendship that has caught fire.
It is quiet understanding, mutual confidence,
sharing and forgiving.
It is loyalty through good and bad times.
It settles for less than perfection
and makes allowances for human weaknesses."*
—Ann Landers

There are types of partners. There is the supplier, vendor type of partner that hooks us up with product to offer our customers. There are support partners that make it easier for us to do business, such as our bank, credit card processors, shipping carriers, third party software companies, hardware companies, and even the snow removal company that cleans our parking lots. All are important. We wanted to be the kind of partner you loved to do business with. We wanted to enhance our relationships with them and to make sure we were a good fit for each other.

Sometimes, in the pursuit of profit, a business relationship with a partner can be a tug of war. Instead of a true partnership, with each understanding the other's needs and taking actions to help each other, it becomes a battle of power and of doing whatever it takes to get a better deal with no regard for the other's interest. Sometimes the vendor forgets who the customer is, and sometimes the customer forgets the vendor doesn't have to sell to them. This leads to an endless series of arm-twisting tactics on both sides, such as "give us a better deal or we won't sell your product" and "if you don't put us on the front page, we won't ship in a timely manner" to excluding a vendor from a promotion or a vendor not sharing the release of new product.

We needed to understand our partners, be concerned with their suggestions, and be aware of the big picture of their business, rather than just being concerned with how something affected us. From our initial list we had a good idea of what we could do and what we could stop doing. This was the beginning, and it was something we wanted to continue to enhance. We also needed to understand that, because of some of our practices, we couldn't expect our suppliers to pay for our free return or no restock fee policies. We needed to make them aware that there would be returns, that we needed their help with them since we didn't have a warehouse, and that we would try to reduce returns with great product information, great data, and easy-to-understand order controls.

We also made it a practice to do partner check-ins. In emails, over the phone, or in person, we would ask these questions. Since people in the company interact with our partners in a variety of ways, it was important that everyone be asking these kinds of questions from time to time with whomever they were interacting with.

1. What can RealTruck do to be a better partner?
2. What can RealTruck stop doing to be a better partner?

As with the other principles, getting some feedback was a good place to start. We needed to keep getting it on an ongoing basis. And it needed to come from all areas we interacted with as a company. Some of our greatest automations came from these answers.

CHAPTER 4

H<small>ERE</small> A<small>RE</small> S<small>OME</small> O<small>F</small> T<small>HE</small> T<small>HINGS</small> W<small>E</small> D<small>ID</small> W<small>ITH</small> P<small>ARTNERS</small>.

- Praised partners when they were practicing examples of our guiding principles
- Followed their policies, pricing, payment, returns and so forth even if other companies were not
- Created installation and product demo videos for them
- Shared sales, returns, warranty, and ship damage data with them
- Shared customer reviews with them
- Provided shipping time reports
- Provided product category comparison data
- Provided advertising data
- When requested, would organize their product data for them to use
- When a partner took us out, we paid rather than expecting them to
- Created annual awards for partners who best exemplified our principles as well as best customer service, returns, automation, data geeks, etc.
- Created a partner of the month program
- Called vendors regularly
- Continually asked vendors what we could do for them
- Creating weekly partner training
- Rock-star welcomes for partner visits
- Automated purchase orders
- EDI integrations for speed and reducing paperwork
- Automated purchasing
- Automated order confirmations and tracking
- Automated inventory feeds
- Paid partners early
- Invited partners to some of our parties
- If something was returned that wasn't resellable, we didn't expect the partner to pay for it
- Visited partner facilities
- Send annual thank you cards
- Created a new vendor onboarding team
- Created a vendor relations team
- Surprised them with RT swag (fuzzy dice, shirts)
- Sent personalized "You're Awesome" cards

Above are examples of some of the things we were doing and, like all things, were subject to ongoing improvement and revaluation. Our suppliers and business partners often would dread traveling to companies across the U.S. and abroad, so you can imagine their expectations about flying into North Dakota. Our team met regularly and worked hard to think of ways to make the experience special, something they would not only remember, but they would talk about with others when they returned home or met with their other clients. This is how, kind of by accident, we created a reputation of being a great company to do business with.

We started with giving partners that visited us a little gift. Since we were in North Dakota, we decided to give gift packs with products that were made from North Dakota. People were surprised and excited by their swag bags of goodies. This continued, but then we added to it.

On a partner visit it occurred to me that, in my younger years when I was a traveling sales rep, I would often mail a book after a visit to business partner and thank them for their time, and add a personal note about something I learned from them. Since RealTruck had a book library, it made sense to give the visitor a book that personally impacted me that I thought they might enjoy. So the RealTruck crew at both offices continued this and then added to it.

Next thing you know, someone put up an easel in the entryway and drew a happy face along with "Welcome Bennett from Husky Liners" on it. Then...

It was a particularly cold day in North Dakota, like -20 degrees, and we had a couple partners coming in from southern California. Someone had the idea to have everyone clap and cheer when they entered the building as that might warm them up a little faster. When they entered the office, everyone stood up, clapped, cheered,

Welcoming The Husky Liners Crew to RT

hooted, and hollered. Our visitors smiled and started to hug some of the staff close to them. I don't think they stopped smiling until they left the building. It was amazing to experience. A side benefit was the staff seemed uplifted as well. This eventually became known as a "Rock-star Welcome."

Over time we added a bubble machine to their grand entrance and we created rock-star welcome videos that we blasted out to social media and shared with the partner. Talk about feeling special. We had partners say, "I have traveled all over the world and this is the best trip I have ever had. I really did not expect this in North Dakota."

We had an office full of creative people, and so it was only natural that this continued to evolve. We had slam-dunk contest welcomes, putting contest welcomes, royal red carpet welcomes, and more.

Our team continued to challenge ourselves to come up with new ways to deliver more to our partners. We wanted our partners to want to work with us, to love us, and to want us as customers.

Some of the results:
- Partners gave us better deals
- Partners gave us first access to new products
- Partners would create training just for us
- Partners would line up to visit
- Partners would put us at the front of the line for processing orders
- Partners would give us awards for customer of the year
- Partners would invite us to visit
- Partners would ask us to carry their products
- Partners would ask us how we created our culture

There were times we had more partners wanting to do business with us than we had time to take on. We would get better at that as we went. From all fronts, we were getting feedback that our partners loved doing business with us. Please don't get the impression that every single partner we had loved us. Like all relationships, sometimes we would fall short. But we had the proper spirit in place to quickly find these stumbling points and try to find a working solution. We also needed to be aware that sometimes, even though a partner might be great company, we might not be the ideal customer for them. If a partner wasn't good at drop shipping, we wouldn't be a good fit for them, they weren't going to be a very good fit for us, and we should part ways.

When I attended the annual SEMA show and saw our partners, my heart would be warmed with some of the things they would say about the people at RealTruck. I was taken aback with how deep and wide-spread the positive comments and color-ful stories about people were in all the depart-ments at RealTruck, from accounting and customer service to marketing and web development. I could feel the friendship, see the joy, and hear the loyalty with the vari-ous relationships they had with the people of RealTruck. RealTruck was becoming a "good" brand and a company they loved.

A partner might be greeted like this

...

Having fun in a partners booth at Sema

Someone in this video conference is getting a Deliver More bracelet

Deliver More poster

Justin & Josh Deltener getting some birthday love

5
TRANSPARENCY ROCKS

"A lack of transparency results in distrust and a deep sense of insecurity." —Dalai Lama

*"It's a matter of trust
It's always been a matter of trust
It's a matter of trust
Cause it's always been a matter of trust."
—Billy Joel*

We value strong and lasting relationships. It is critical for relationship-building to have effective, open, and honest communication. Communication is always difficult in any organization, being transparent eliminates guesswork and misunderstanding. We want everyone to always try to go to any length to encourage transparent, thorough, complete, and effective communication. Everyone needs to understand how each of us and our teams connect to the big picture and what our mission is. Clear and honest communication, guided by transparency, allows us to create stronger, lasting relationships and positive emotional experiences with our customers, partners, teams and each other. Work takes on new meaning, instead of a task or chore; we are now doing something for a friend. We are able to transmit a genuine attitude of caring that translates into service made visible.

2. Transparency Rocks

We were an e-commerce company from conservative North Dakota living in a very social world. North Dakota has lots of hard-working folk. Sometimes a little too close to the vest with their feelings, which can create a bootstraps mentality. Be strong, work hard, and keep your feelings to yourself, thank you. They will give you the shirt off their back and not want anything in return. If you walked into most businesses here, you might have a hard time figuring out who owns the place or who the manager is. Their car, office, and how they dressed would be the same as the rest of the employees. Most are proper and polite from a distance. If you had some ink on your cheek, they wouldn't want to be rude and tell you. If you gave them bad service, to be polite, they may not say anything.

Again, this wasn't 100% across the board, but if we were to grow and improve, we had to have a high level of transparency. Lack of transparency creates distrust and fear. Fear prevents people from doing what is right. Reduce fear and you increase doing what is right. Lack of or poor and ineffective communication creates fears, and fears are the seeds of rumors.

Most of us get the basic concept of communication—verbal, written, and so forth. But there's another very important aspect which is often overlooked, and that is making sure the person we are communicating with truly understands what we are trying to communicate. We need to check in, beyond just asking "make sense?" Sometimes distrust arises because of failure to communicate in a timely manner.

Here's an example of not being transparent. Jeff, Lucy Geigle, our chief people officer, and Debi, our customer service manager, had a meeting. We were running out of space. We made the decision to expand the offices. Next thing you know, contractors are swinging hammers upstairs. The plan was to move me and the product line managers upstairs and that would make room for additional customer service reps. This would allow all the customer service reps to stay together.

A few days later I heard that there would be no raise for two years because we were remodeling a "grand" style 10,000 square foot office for me up stairs. I was aghast. The entire floor? And because of the expense no raises? Wow. I wondered who was putting out bad info. After some investigating, it turned out someone said that they thought I was moving my office upstairs. The next person made the assumption that it was just me moving up there. They passed that on to someone who was wondering why all the contractors were upstairs. That person shared with another person, who wondered if we were leasing the entire floor, which came back as we were. Then next person ascertained from the tidbits that we were building a huge office upstairs just for Scott and shared this with another person, upon which the person next to them commented, "Oh, the boss gets a grand 10,000 square foot office. I suppose now we won't get any raises for years."

Needless to say, by the time it got back to me, I was all wonky and negative. This could have been prevented if we had taken the time to explain that because of rapid growth we were renting the upstairs and would be building additional workspaces. That would have resulted in everyone knowing what was going on and way less fear and assumptions.

Sometimes an employee would approach me and share a frustration. It might be something as simple as a mouse or a computer issue. They would say, "My mouse is glitchy, which is making it hard to get any work done, and no one will get me a new one."

I would ask them, "Did you talk to your boss about it?"

No.

"Did you ask IT if they would get you one?"

No.

Then they would say something like, "I shouldn't have to. The company doesn't seem to care if I have the proper tools. Plus, if they were a good boss or IT was doing a good job, they would know it's not working properly, but clearly they don't care."

"Hmmmm, is it possible that they don't watch you that closely?"

I suppose.

"Is it possible that if you asked for help, they might care? You are blaming your boss, IT, and the company for your mouse not working, when you haven't been transparent enough to ask for help with overcoming an obstacle that they are not even aware you have. Those are some expectations no company, boss or department can possibly meet. Ask for help. Share what you need and why. If for some reason they can't help you, try to understand where they are coming from."

People at a company often feel like they never know what is going on and they are not appreciated. Deliver More and Be Humble really helped with people feeling appreciation. And Transparency Rocks really helps with trust and feeling like you know what is going on. It helps with seeing how an individual fits into the big picture and creates trust. You always hear that communication is a two-way street. That is true, but how do you create it? How do you actually do it, or practice doing it? The best way is to start with questions.

START WITH QUESTIONS

> **"***There is a difference between listening and waiting for your turn to speak.***" —***Simon Sinek***

Like Delivering More, we started with questions. Here are some of them:
1. How can I be more transparent with my boss, reports, and coworkers?
2. How can I be more transparent with customers and partners?
3. How can RealTruck be more transparent with customers, partners, and employees?

Ask your boss, direct-reports, and coworkers these questions. Do it more than once. Do it fairly regularly.
1. How can I be a better employee?
2. How can I be a better boss?
3. How can I be a better coworker / teammate?

Then shut up and listen. Don't correct them with "the facts" or "reality." Just listen. You will learn some things about yourself and what you can do to be better. Some feedback will be spot on and some not so much. They may ask those same questions back to you. Then share your thoughts, ideally in a helpful manner. Trust is the key to closeness and transparency is the door of trust.

Once we started asking these questions, the answers started coming. Over time, we could see employees connecting more and more with each other, with customers, and with our partners. The increase in trust could be felt. This closeness was heartwarming. Please don't get the impression we found transparent perfection; rather, we were progressing in a more and more transparent direction. This guiding principle was certainly the most challenging to practice. It was also sometimes the hardest to see. This is where our practice of employees shouting others out for practicing this principle really helped get it going inside our culture. Recognizing it is just as important as trying to practice it. Fear begins to turn into trust. Apathy turns into a feeling of appreciation.

It's Ok To posters

TRANSPARENCY ROCKS ACTIONS

As with all of the guiding principles, some of things we did were enhanced and improved over time, and others reduced or in some cases stopped altogether because of how they tied into the guiding principles. Here's a list of some of the transparent things we did.

- Shared sales and profit numbers company wide
- Anyone could see daily sales in real time anytime
- Established an ask anything policy
- Regular team and manager meetings
- Shared product sales, returns, and warranty reports company wide
- Established key metrics by department and shared company wide
- Shared traffic, sales, returns, ship damage, and warranty reports with partners

- Stopped offering coupon codes
- Stopped discounting over the phones
- Stopped accepting spiffs from partners to push their products
- Published all customer reviews on a product (whether the manufacturer liked it or not)
- Displayed our popular products by popularity, not by which ones we made the most on
- Displayed real estimated shipping times
- Conducted town halls
- Created a culture team
- Employee profiles on front and back side of website
- What's up videos
- Managers and team leaders could take employees out to chat or for lunch at the company expense at any time
- Employees were given the opportunity to evaluate their managers
- Regular reviews that evaluated how well the guiding principles were being practiced
- Transparent job postings
- Transparent job interviews
- Team members included in hiring interviews
- Transparent customer reviews
- Transparent shipping dates
- Transparent meetings
- HR shared benefit costs
- HR annual total compensation report for each employee

For Transparency Rocks, I did a fairly regular "What's up at RT" video and the content came from the 9@9 managers meeting. Everyone in the company felt like they knew what was going on. Web development and IT from time to time would do tech tip videos or how-to videos and would share them with the company. Over time, marketing would do a what's up video and the culture team would do that same. It was always a platform used to pass on ideas, attitudes, and actions for enhancing our guiding principles or also to clear up any confusion.

ASK ANYTHING INITIATIVE

We added an *ask anything* initiative. Folks could anonymously ask anything by submitting a question and they would be answered by me or whomever I felt in the best position to answer the question. We had boxes around the office for these questions and also, on the backside of the website, people could ask a question anonymously. That question would be emailed to me. Justin coded it in a way that no one would know who asked it, not even the developers. The question and answer were shared with the entire company. We received questions from anything from why aren't we using Outlook mail anymore to why does such and such manager take 90 minutes for lunch? The only editing we did was to remove identifiers if someone used someone's name or if it was someone calling someone else out specifically. If someone used one of the ask anything tools and called out a person by name, the question and answer would be shared omitting the person who was called out and any reference that would indicate who asked it or who it was about.

Someone asked, "Why does Fred, who's supposed to be our supervisor, always take 90 minute lunches? That seems like favoritism and nobody seems to do anything about it." Or "Why is Betty, who has been late for her shift twice this week, not getting in trouble for it? When I was late once, my boss spoke to me about it right away. Why isn't Betty getting a talking to? Thanks, Jennifer." Those two questions would be answered like this:

Question: "Why does X, who's supposed to be our supervisor, always take 90 minute lunches?

Answer: "Our supervisors are empowered to use their time how they see fit. Often a manager, supervisor, or team lead may be doing things for us before and after work that we may not always see. Sometimes they may take a longer lunch for business or even personal reasons. We trust them. If they are taking advantage of the company, we believe it will shake out over time in other areas. In the spirit of transparency and taking risks, I encourage you to ask them. Their answer may surprise you."

Question: "Snoopy has been late for his shift twice this week. When I was late once, my boss spoke to me about it right away. Why isn't Snoopy getting a talking to?"

Answer: "We trust the boss will address this issue with the employee. When it comes to employee coaching and discipline, because of employee privacy, the reasons, plans and consequences related to an individual employee often are not shared publicly. Trust that the boss is working with the employee even though you may not see this directly. If the employee corrects the tardiness, great. If they do not, well, then this will be reflected in their reviews and ultimately result in their loss of employment. Last, it's also possible the employee made arrangements in advance with their boss that they would be late. Thanks for asking the question."

Initially, I answered most of the ask anything questions. Over time, this was passed on to other leaders in the company. The ask anything policy was great for a few things. We got some great questions. We got some very challenging questions. Sometimes the answers weren't perfect or 100% spot on all the time, but everyone got them. It was a great outlet for clearing up confusion, discovering conflicting policies, and helping us all get on the same page faster.

And yes, once in a while we would get some weird or inappropriate questions, such as "Why does X, who is in some of our product videos, drive a shitty-looking truck around town? It's old, rusty, and it makes us look bad." I wanted to say, "Why don't you ask him? You might learn that it's a lifelong rebuild project, a pickup he loves. A pickup that survived the flood he was in a few years earlier."

I didn't share this question or answer because there wasn't a way to hide his identity at the time. But this led to doing employee profiles, where employees could be interviewed and say more about themselves to everyone in the company. Ask anything is meant to ask questions that you can't find answers for. To be used to understand some of the "why we do what we dos" and to make sure any question can get to our leaders, while protecting the anonymity of the asker.

In addition, we tried to do town halls at each office a couple of times a year to allow folks to ask questions of the leaders of the company. These could be challenging to coordinate, given we already had lots of folks on the phone, working a variety of shifts. We would generally shut down the phones for a few hours, and turn on a greeting for the phones that we were having an employee town hall and would be back in a couple hours. We would have the town hall in the afternoons and ask the evening and weekend shifts to come if at all possible.

Employee Profile
Ben Sailer

- I'm half English and grew up in a military family living all over the UK and the US.
- I listen to a lot of punk bands and shoot a lot of concert photos
- Archer and The Walking Dead are the only reasons I'd consider getting cable. And Mad Men. I love Mad Men.
- I run a lot and want to do at least one 5k this summer.
- My niece and nephew are pretty rad little people.

Ben having fun with his employee profile

For customers, transparency was important as well. We discovered that at some point, our product categories that were filtered by "best sellers" was actually coded to show what RT made the best margins on. So we either needed to change the sort name to "What RT makes the most money on" or change it truly to be best sellers based on unit count and dollars, which we did. This is an example of someone wanting to help the company sell more of what we had the best margins on, which isn't by itself bad. However, that little snippet of code was in conflict with our guiding principle, and once we became aware, it was a no-brainer to everyone as to why we should fix it. As for how to better increase our margins, that would be something our other guiding principles could help with, while sacrificing transparency.

For customers, as mentioned before, we removed coupon codes and jump-through-hoop promotions. We wanted to be very clear about our pricing, what they were getting, and what it cost without hidden fees or return policies written like a legal document.

We also wanted to be transparent with shipping times while also delivering more to our customers. If a product would normally ship in a day, we would list two days to make sure we always shipped when we said we would or sooner. Yes, some other competitors would fudge their ship times to get a sale, knowing a product normally doesn't ship for two days and listing one day to get the sale, but we didn't want to do this; that would clearly be in conflict with our principles. We knew we might give up some sales, but we wanted to make sure we would keep our word. Along with transparency, that was more important than getting a sale. Since we were drop shipping everything, we could only use historical data and inventory feeds to know when something generally ships, so we added a day of padding to make sure we kept our word on when it would ship out. We also knew if we shipped on time or sooner than expected, it would create a memorable experience.

For product reviews, we published all of them, good or bad, as long as the product review was about the product and not us or the shipping carrier. Sometimes if RealTruck failed or a shipping carrier failed, the customer would share that in the product review, which should be their review of the product, not us or the shipping carrier. It would not be fair for a product to be rated poorly if RT or the shipping carrier had failed. So those were not published, but anything else was fair game. Sometimes the vendors would call and ask us to remove a bad review, but we would not. Sharing with them supported our principle of transparency. This led to our sharing return, review, warranty, and shipping damage data with our partners to help them improve their products and processes.

This practice of sharing sales data and return data with our vendors for their brand and summary data for the categories on products they took a part of created more trust. It's also why they often gave us first access to new products, images, and data. Trust works both ways. They would see how we were doing with their products, give us feedback on what they thought we could do better, and also be empowered to improve their products based on the return, warranty, missing parts, and ship damage data.

We stopped taking spiffs from vendors. Vendors would often give extra money or gifts to people on the phone if we pushed their product. We would not accept this as it did not align with providing a great customer experience or with being transparent. Unless of course somehow on the web and over the phone we could tell them "Hey, we are making extra cash if you buy this," which wasn't something we wanted to do. So we stopped accepting these payments, which was unheard of in our industry. Our partners' real goal was to grow their sales with us.

In the early days of RealTruck, we did allow spiffs. It was always a bad deal. What would happen is, an employee would push that product. The vendor would pay say $10 a unit for every one they sold. Sometimes the employee would do about anything to sell the product so they could get the extra $10. They would discount the product to sell it. They would sometimes sell a customer on something they didn't want. Employees on the phone would fight over who talked to the customer first and who should get credit for a sale to get the spiff. RealTruck would make less money because of the discounting, and customers would lose a little trust in us as to whether we were helpful or not. Employees might make a little extra cash, but at the expense of our margins, which effects everyone at RealTruck.

Plus, I think it also took away from some of their credibility because one day they would push one product, saying it's the greatest, and the next day or week they'd say the same thing about a different brand that had the same kind of product, because that other brand now had a spiff. And the partner was hurt because they might have gotten a small pump in sales, but no real long-term brand growth. So our principle of transparency made it very easy to stop accepting spiffs from a partner.

We came up with a better solution for this that helped the partner, us, and our customers: a partner of the month program where we would focus on that partner and their products company wide. As for spiffs, the only thing close that we could accept would be company-wide prizes such as a pizza party or something that everyone benefited from if we hit certain goals with that brand. Ideally they would do some extra training and visit onsite for the party. A partner doing a company wide pizza party for us created some fun that everyone benefited from and helped put some energy into growing that brand as a whole, rather than incentivising an individual person and an individual product. Plus, sharing with the world that a partner threw a pizza party for us because we grew their brand seemed a lot better than adding a disclaimer to the website that said, "If you talk to a person about this product, they are getting an extra $10 to sell it to you."

Everyone at RealTruck had ready access to all our sales info. Daily sales, sales by product, sales by brand, returns, warranty, ship damage, and so forth. Everyone was engaged in knowing how well we were doing. We also shared monthly, quarterly, and annual summary reports of our progress for everyone to read. We had an entire company of folks paying attention to sales, margins, returns, and so on rather than just marketing and finance. This was huge for creating employee trust with the company. It was also very helpful in finding solutions for problems from all areas of the company.

WHY IS TRANSPARENCY IMPORTANT?

Transparency leads to trust. It increases engagement and ultimately reduces fear. We wanted open and honest communication without guesswork. Communication works both ways. It's important we make sure those we are communicating with understand what we truly mean. It's ok to ask questions. We are closest to those with whom we feel we can speak and share freely. It's important we move in that direction with customers, partners, and each other within the company.

We learned when an employee had an issue to ask questions such as, did you talk with your supervisor about that? Often the answer was no. How can your boss help, if you don't ask? Often folks think their boss knows and sees all or sometimes knows or sees nothing. In either case, it is never black and white. If you share with your boss a problem, solution, idea, or something you want to do personally or professionally, most will do whatever they can to help.

In human resources, we started creating more transparent job postings, job descriptions, interviews, benefits cost sharing, and even "Why work at Real-Truck" videos. More of this will be discussed in "Include Fun," but ultimately in HR we started asking if what we were doing was transparent and asking how we could be more transparent. Anything was up for discussion and review. For interviews, especially after we started to move towards practicing the guiding principles that culture fit interviews, we realized this had to be done first. Then if they passed that, we brought them back to do a skill set interview. To be transparent with the candidates, we let them know what was coming in advance. Seems obvious now, but deliver more, improve, include fun, and take risks often move faster than transparency. For job postings, we tried to be real and include the culture in them. After all, if you aren't okay working next to someone wearing clown shoes, then RealTruck probably wouldn't be a good fit for you.

It was important that we tried be honest and realistic about our culture in our postings and interviews. We started a RealTruck Basics for new hires. Anyone who was hired, whether for customer service or for accounting, would go

Townhall fun

through it. Upon graduating there would be a basic training T-shirt along with a hooray from the entire staff at the main office. That too was important we convey to those we interviewed.

With the help of accounting, HR also started doing annual total compensation reports that included the standard stuff like wages, health insurance, and 401k, but also included other benefits and expenses such as the cost of coffee and snacks per person, cost of the company parties per person, and so forth. This helped employees see beyond what their more obvious compensation was and tried to capture all the benefits at RealTruck.

Accounting would of course share the official traditional numbers of sales and expenses along with profit for quarterly profit sharing, but we would also pass on tips on tax savings, cost-cutting ideas, areas where we could save money, and other financial opportunities to help the company.

Accounting was helpful with explaining margin, what capital purchases were, and how they affect the bottom line. Helping brand managers understand how sometimes discounting a product 10% at the top can cut the profit margin of a product by 50% or even turn it into a loss. This was accomplished by showing them how to properly calculate margin. Profitability is often most affected by how well you buy. Meaning, you can't really control the street price that much. If you have great service, perhaps you can charge a little bit more. But ultimately, how well you buy affects it more. Accounting helped everyone understand all the various buying

Shawn doing his famous pose, #TheShawn

discounts a partner might have available such as base discount, early payment discounts, ad-coop credits, volume discounts, quarterly or annual rebates, and so forth, along with the effect of returns on a given brand's overall performance. Accounting worked with web development to make all of these needs viewable to anyone at RealTruck in real time by brand, category, and so forth. We often would get better discounts just by asking this simple question of each partner occasionally: "Is there anything we can do to get a better discount?" Most would give us an answer and if we could do it, we would.

Departments all across the company grew in their level of transparency, from marketing to the brands team better communicating new products and processes inside and outside of the company. Marketing was great about helping communicate, often in an over-the-top fun manner, examples of how to and how not to practice our principles.

...

A little finger painting during basic training

Transparency Rocks poster

Transparency helped develop closer relationships with business partners; Scott with Bob Tyler, founder of Husky Liners

Josh giving Jeff a Transparency Rocks bracelet

Katie enjoying the no dress code policy with her Zubaz

6
IMPROVE

"Progress is impossible without change, and those who cannot change their minds cannot change anything." —George Bernard Shaw

"It's been a long, a long time coming. But I know a change gonna come, oh yes it will.." —Sam Cooke

With an open mind and a passionate spirit, we pursued innovation and ongoing improvement. We wrapped our hearts and minds around the idea of ongoing change. We created it, drove it, embraced it, inspired it and lead it. Status quo is the curse of business and we wanted to be extraordinary. Constant change is something we sought. Not only did we seek change, we wanted to be the creators of it. Companies could copy our policies and ideas, but they couldn't copy our people or our spirit. Innovation had to come from everywhere in our company.

3. Improve

We found ways to do more with less by always remembering "good enough" is the enemy of the great. Each of us needed to spend time learning new things personally and professionally for ongoing improvement. Working hard and putting in the extra effort is what creates great transformation. We were adventurous and always strove to make something better.

WHAT NEEDS TO CHANGE?

Everything is in a constant state of change. We really needed to get our hearts and minds around embracing, creating, and driving change. This idea of embracing ongoing change is the backbone for killing status quo, improving operational efficiencies, and of course personal growth. But to get there, we had to increase our open-mindedness by being very receptive to new ideas and asking lots of questions. We needed to make time for learning, be willing to try new things, look at those results, and repeat. Often, asking why are we doing this is the starting point.

WHY ARE WE DOING THIS?

> "*All the great organizations in the world, all have a sense of why that organization does what it does.*"
> —*Simon Sinek*

We had to always be asking why we were doing something. Just because something was ingrained into the culture didn't mean it couldn't be changed. Anything was up to be changed if it needed to improve.

A little story I often told is about a young boy and his mother. Little Jonny asks his mom why she always cuts the corner off the ham of before she cooks it. Mom says, "I don't know, that's how we've always done it. That's how grandma showed me when she was teaching me to cook."

Little Jonny was a inquisitive kid. He called Grandma to ask, why does my mom cut the corner off of the ham before she cooks it? Grandma chuckles a little and says, "I'm not sure why your mom does it, but I did it once when the ham was too big to fit in the pan." This story has two main points. One is, we should know why we are doing something, and the answer has to be better than "that's how I was shown to do it" or "that's how we have always done it." The second is to always ask why we are doing something. The answer may have fit in the past, but does not apply now.

Innovation creation starts from questions. It evolves to learning, testing, doing, and repeating. Doing more with less is a result of creative innovation. This can't fall on one person or team in an organization. Yes, we need leaders. We need decision makers. Often the wants and problems that most need to be solved and the initial idea of a solution come from the front lines. Transparency allows for information flow, but a company of open-minded people is needed to embrace ongoing change and improvement. Our guiding principle of taking risks is our power and permission to create change.

This principle of improvement also included personal growth and learning. Most of us want to learn and grow. The clamors of life, making a living, having a little fun often interfere with this desire to learn and grow, unless you are the highly disciplined type who makes regular time to learn something new. It was clear we needed to create a culture where making time to learn is important, whatever the learning might be. If someone learned something new, whether something personal such as yoga or something that helped them at work, such as speaking Spanish, we praised them for it. We challenged everyone and all departments to grow and improve personally and professionally.

Jenn and Tami started in CS and moved up to OFS Lead & Brand Manager

Liberty graduating RT basic training

THE ROLL OUT

66*If your time to you is worth savin'*
Then you better start swimmin'
Or you'll sink like a stone
For the times they are a-changin'."
—*Tracy Chapman*

Like Deliver More and Transparency Rocks, this guiding principle was rolled out to the company after Transparency Rocks, and we focused on it for two months to get it going in our culture. Each department got together and we started with questions. Some of the why and what questions needed to be asked from a given department's perspective.

Here are some of the general questions we started asking company wide:
- What could we do better?
- What should we do more of?
- What should we do less of?
- What should we stop doing?
- Why are we doing what we are doing, and the answer can't be "because we always have done it that way."
- When is the last time I have learned something new personally? Professionally?
- When is the last time I was open to a new idea?
- When something is new, do I look for why it may be better or why it won't work?
- What practices do we have that don't align with our guiding principles?
- Do I see any waste in the company or my department? What can be done about it?
- What are three things the company could do to save money?
- What are three things I could do to save money?
- What are three things I would like to learn?
- What is stopping me from learning these three things?
- What are three things that would make my job more rewarding?

Here are some of the department-specific questions:

CUSTOMER SERVICE

- What can we do to improve customer service?
- Where are we falling short on Delivering More?
- Where are we falling short on Transparency Rocks?
- What are we doing over and over again that could be automated?
- When is the last time I learned something new about customer service?
- What are three things I could do to be more effective or efficient?
- What would I like more training on?
- What tools or resources do I need that I don't have?
- What tools or resources do our customers or partners need that they don't have?
- Why is great customer service important to me?

ACCOUNTING

- What can we do to improve the accounting department?
- Where are we falling short on Delivering More?
- Where are we falling short on Transparency Rocks?
- What are we doing over and over again that could be automated?
- When is the last time I learned something new about accounting?
- What are three things I could do to be more effective or efficient?
- What would I like more training on?
- What tools or resources do I need that I don't have?
- What tools or resources do our customers or partners need that they don't have?
- Why is doing good work important to me?

ORDER FULFILLMENT

- What can we do to improve the order fulfillment department?
- Where are we falling short on Delivering More?
- Where are we falling short on Transparency Rocks?
- What are we doing over and over again that could be automated?
- When did I last learn something new about our order processing?
- What are three things I could do to be more effective or efficient?
- What would I like more training on?

- What tools or resources do I need that I don't have?
- What tools or resources do our customers or partners need that they don't have?
- Why is fulfilling orders important to me?
- Web Development / IT
- What can we do to improve our web development / IT?
- Where are we falling short on Delivering More?
- Where are we falling short on Transparency Rocks?
- What are we doing over and over again that could be automated?
- When is the last time I learned something new related to my job?
- What are three things I could do to be more effective or efficient?
- What would I like more training on?
- What tools or resources do I need that I don't have?
- What tools or resources do our customers or partners need that they don't have?
- Why is web development or IT work important to me?
- Marketing
- What can we do to improve our marketing internally and externally?
- Where are we falling short on Delivering More?
- Where are we falling short on Transparency Rocks?
- What are we doing over and over again that could be automated?
- When is the last time I learned something new related to marketing?
- What are three things I could do to be more effective or efficient?
- What would I like more training on?
- What tools or resources do I need that I don't have?
- What tools or resources do our customers or partners need that they don't have?
- Why is our marketing work important to me?

MERCHANDISING / VENDOR RELATIONS

- What can we do to improve the our partner relationships?
- Where are we falling short on Delivering More?
- Where are we falling short on Transparency Rocks?
- What are we doing over and over again that could be automated?
- When is the last time I learned something new related to my job?
- What are three things I could do to be more effective or efficient?
- What would I like more training on?

- What tools or resources do I need that I don't have?
- What tools or resources do our partners need that they don't have?
- Why is working with brands and partners important to me?

HUMAN RESOURCES

- What can we do to improve our HR department?
- Where are we falling short on Delivering More?
- Where are we falling short on Transparency Rocks?
- What are we doing over and over again that could be automated?
- When is the last time I learned something new related to HR?
- What are three things I could do to be more effective or efficient?
- What would I like more training on?
- What tools or resources do I need that I don't have?
- What tools or resources do our current or future employees need that they don't have?
- Why are our people important to me?

From a cultural perspective, just laying the foundation of "question everything" was very powerful. Anything could be changed. We wanted to have a really great customer experience, we wanted our partners to love us, and we wanted our employees to know we cared about them. So the guiding principle to "Improve" was paramount.

WHINER: NOTHING EVER GETS DONE WITHOUT ME

What began to happen was, departments and teams would meet and go over the questions and answers. These would be summarized and shared company wide. One of my ongoing "whines" to Jeff and Justin was that it seemed like nothing ever got executed without me being directly involved. This wasn't totally true; a great deal of it was my perception. My desire was to be needed and wanted. Some of it was lack of awareness. Some of it was also very true. This principle was the first hammer that helped destroy my complaint. The second was our guiding principle of Taking Risks. People were now beginning to feel empowered to ask why we do what we do. They were empowered to even question me, whether directly or through an ask anything tool. Better yet, everyone was empowered to create change and learn without asking me if it was ok. That's not to say sometimes things were changed for the worse or without taking other people, departments, or the entire company into account. Those things happened. But we got better at looking at the big picture and asking if this change would fit with our guiding principles. It was a process that never stopped.

The shout outs going around the company from the What's Up at RT videos, along with employees in every area praising each other, helped us all really see this guiding principle in action, whether someone got complimented for learning yoga or because someone changed the way we handled a return process. It really helped everyone see that anything could be changed and questioned, along with knowing old dogs can learn new tricks with the push to learn and grow personally and professionally. Anything we automated along the way was shouted out, sometimes just one person and other times an entire team.

Here is a story on change and why sometimes the "stop doing" list is more important than the "start doing" list. This is one of the first things that came about because of this principle.

One day I popped into the office and Bonnie, who was in reception, had a two-foot tall stack of invoices from our vendors on her desk. She was stamping a date received on each copy. Accounting was short-handed. Being a drop ship company means, for every order received from a customer, that we created one or more purchase orders that we would then send to a vendor to fill. The vendor shipped it and they would mail or email the invoice to be paid. Terms of payment varied, but most had a 2% to 3% discount if we paid the invoice within 10 days. So if we had 2,500 orders a week, and the average order had 1.5 items, that could mean 3,750 invoices from vendors a week, or about 195,000 a year. If 80% have early pay discounts, that would mean we were stamping 156,000 or so invoices a year or 600 a day for a five-day work week.

I asked Bonnie why she was stamping the invoices with a date received. She didn't know but would find out. The next day, when I got to work, Bonnie shared that we were stamping the invoices that had early pay discounts. We always took advantage of early pay discounts. It's just good business sense. We were stamping these early pay discount invoices so we would know the exact date we received the bill, and if a vendor refused to give us a early pay discount because of mail delay, we would be able to show them the date we received the invoice.

Everyone helping on the phones for busy season—even me

Next question: how many times has a vendor refused to give us an early pay discount because they believed we were late? Bonnie wasn't sure but said she would find out. Day three, Bonnie comes rushing up to share the good news. We were no longer going to be stamping invoices with a date received. "Why?" I asked. Turns out we never had a vendor refuse an early pay discount. We were stamping thousands and thousands of invoices for something that might happen that never had. Furthermore, that awareness prompted someone else to realize that, even if a vendor refused an early pay discount, and we used our stamped date as proof when we received the invoice, the vendor would have to trust us that date we stamped on it was accurate in the first place.

This might seem like an rather ridiculous example, but when employees can't or don't feel empowered to ask why they are doing something, this kind of thing happens all the time. Every time I share the story, there is a part of me that wishes we kept track of how many invoices we actually stamped over the years so I could mathematically calculate how much labor and time was wasted because we never asked why we were doing something. On the plus side, accounting suddenly wasn't short-handed either.

WHAT DID WE CHANGE?

"Leadership and learning are indispensable to each other."
—John F. Kennedy

Everything was up to be changed. Like the other guiding principles, some things we did and continued to try to improve, and other things were scrapped entirely. This was an ongoing process, not a destination. Here are some of the programs, processes, and practices that were developed from this guiding principle:

1. RealTruck University
2. Learn More Earn More
3. Auto PO Bot (90% of orders processed hands-free)
4. Josh-o-rithm (Product Recommendation Engine)
5. Product Line Editor (anyone could add products to the website)
6. Culture Team
7. Vendor Awards
8. Hiring Practices and Processes
9. Real and Fun Job Postings
10. Bulk Product Editor
11. Vehicle Application Editor
12. RealTruck Olympics
13. Marketing Practices
14. Employee and Manager Reviews
15. Guiding Principles Reviews
16. Video Creation Process
17. Truck Builds
18. Dream Space
19. Exercise and Relax Rooms
20. Culture Team Budgets
21. Onsite and Offsite Training
22. Weekly Partner Product Training
23. Team-Building Time
24. RealTruck Basic Training

25. All Hands On Deck Helping Customer Service Black Friday, Cyber Monday to Holidays
26. How RealTruck Works Videos
27. Culture Videos
28. Training Videos for Most Departments
29. Automated Tracking
30. ESD Algorithm
31. Rock-Star Welcomes
32. Themed Potlucks
33. Almost Weekly Dress-up Days
34. No Dress Code—However, we do try to dissuade scuba gear for practical reasons.
35. Decorate Your Area However You Want
36. Personal Development Time
37. Performance Reviews Two Times a Year
38. Guiding Principles Review Tied Into Profit Sharing
39. Department Contests
40. Outside Office Team Building
41. Free Coffee, Tea, and Hot Chocolate
42. Real Product Reviews
43. Random Actions of Kindness Program
44. Guiding Principle Swag
45. Birthday Cards and Cash For Kids
46. Charity Work like Meals On Wheels and Ronald McDonald House
47. Fun Thank You Postcards
48. Employee Street Signs
49. Automated Inventory Feeds
50. Read A Book On The Clock
51. Employee Coaching For Personal or Professional Reasons
52. Expanded Year, Make and Model Displays For Customers

The reality is, the list above is a short list of changes created and enhanced. People were empowered to ask questions and take actions to improve something. It encompassed all areas, from the front and back side of the website to embracing new technologies. Enhancements to our operations, marketing, customer service, returns, merchandising, human resources, web development, and accounting. This seed of continual improvement was spreading everywhere, including to our policies, programs, and processes. We were learning and growing by leaps and bounds.

Sending people to trade shows and encouraging continued education is something most companies try to do. RealTruck was pushing the envelope. We encouraged department leaders to push the bar on training, whether onsite or off-site, and they did. RealTruck basic training was developed. This training was something everyone at RealTruck would go through alongside new hires. It helped folks learn more about our guiding principles, about our culture, and why we do what we do. It also included folks learning about customer service and spending some time on the phones. This would come in handy during Black Friday, Cyber Monday, and the holiday season, where all employees were encouraged and given the opportunity to help support and actively participate directly with customer service. Folks from all departments would cook pancakes and serve them to the customer service teams or they would be on the phones right next to the more experienced customer service reps taking calls.

Our spirit of transparency helped here as well. Clearly, a customer calling during busy seasons who gets someone from marketing, IT, or accounting on the phone isn't going to get the same level of service they would from a fully trained customer service rep. We would encourage helpers to share with the customers what department they normally worked in, that they were helping the customer service team during the busy season, and wanted to help them if they could. If at any point in the call they weren't able to effectively assist them, they would happily get a fully trained customer service rep on the phone. This practice was great all around. It gave folks from all departments a better understanding of what customer service is like.

Often, it spurred development to find better solutions for customers and the customer service team. Folks from web development and IT working on the phones for a little bit became quickly aware of needs the customer service team and customer had that could be easily enhanced and improved with some development or new technology. Marketing got a better understanding on how over-promising and not properly managing our marketing expectations can get a customer upset or customer service in a jackpot.

Accounting folks developed more empathy and understanding of the pressures and joys of working directly with customers. Traditionally, accounting people might see the customer service team as screwing off at work a bit too much. After a day or two on the phone, this attitude is dramatically reshaped. It's a little easier to understand why someone from customer

Resa, Jenny & Jenn—3 of 4 on the OFS Team

Meet The Team postcards

Making RT parties better

service might blow off a little frustration by walking around the office aimlessly, doing jumping jacks, creating a better-performing paper airplane, jamming to some music, telling a joke that gets everyone laughing, or taking a trip to the relax room. This was all topped off by having massages available that someone could sign up for along with breakfast, lunch, supper and snack requests being fulfilled by people from various departments. Nothing like seeing the VP of Operations or a brand manager taking a food order for a customer service rep and then delivering it to them with a smile. It was powerful to see.

We also started doing company-wide culture surveys to assess how we were doing and what we needed to put more attention on. The first assessment showed we were weak at giving back to the community, that our leaders weren't as transparent as the rest of the staff, and that employees felt they had more work than they were able to get done. The transparency weakness is what created the ask anything program, the town halls, and managers empowered to do on- and off-site team building activities.

As for giving back to the community, once we became aware of the company-wide desire to do more in that area, the folks of RealTruck took action. That led to a pick-a-charity program, where we picked a charity of the

"Big Red" truck photo shoot

month or the quarter and raised money for it, which the company generally matched. It also led to getting involved with Meals on Wheels, the Anne Carlsen Center, the Ronald McDonald House, an annual food drive and more.

One of my favorites was when we created a random acts of kindness program. It started as an external thing. A few of us picked people or places in town and we would each do something to show we appreciated them. I delivered a few dozen boxes of donuts to all the folks who worked at the city dump. I shared with the manager and a couple of the crew that I appreciate them for what they do for the community, and also left a note on each of the boxes. Yes, I got some weird looks, but I felt really good. I bought boxes of Skittles, added a "Just wanted to let you know you're awesome" sticker on them, and spent a few hours going around town and handing them out to folks. I would go up to someone and say, thank you for doing what you do, give them the Skittles, and watch them smile big after they read the note.

This random act of kindness concept expanded to where someone at RealTruck created a jar full of ideas where you would grab one from the jar and then go do it. Things like "go out of your way to give someone you don't know a compliment" or "do something for someone to show how much you appreci-

Having some fun at the Sema Show

ate them." These kinds of things have a ripple effect and also really encompass aspects of all our guiding principles. We even had lollipops and cans of soda pop with compliments on them that you could give to someone at one point.

One of the things that developed was the "Learn more, Earn more" program, where the customer service reps could earn more faster, if they learned more. The more skills you had around customer service, returns, order fulfillment, product knowledge, reception, and basic accounting, the more you could make. Your compensation wasn't determined by whether your boss liked you or not, rather how much you knew how to do. This program was for folks in customer service, returns, order fulfillment, and reception.

If you had all these skills, you could literally do everything to take care of a customer, from helping them place the order, purchasing it from a vendor, creating a return, requesting a return authorization from the vendor, getting it shipped back, refunding the customer, and requesting the vendor credit. You would understand the work involved from start to finish as well as appreciate the need to help the customer get the best product for them and their needs the first time. How many skills you had that enhanced your ability to do your job was what mattered.

No matter what area you actually worked within, those departments allowed you to do better because you understood and could do all the jobs in the process. The long term goal was that this would be where our product merchandisers and brand managers would come from. Since we were growing, we had a big need to get more product merchandisers and brand managers. Getting them from the front lines, totally understanding the entire customer process, made for great merchandisers and brand managers. They really had a good understanding of why it was important to find and work with partners that were not only willing, but also capable of doing business with a drop ship company like us. Almost all of the brand manager and merchandiser teams came from the front lines. It made me very proud when I would see a job ad from RealTruck that included opportunity for advancement. It wasn't just job ad fluff; it was something we really practiced.

In the beginning we were really pushing the crew to read the four core books, on their time or company time. If someone wasn't much of a reader, we would encourage them to at least read the chapter summaries. We located YouTube videos of the authors discussing the books that we shared out for all to watch. We also had meetings to discuss what we learned from a book and how we could apply that to what we were doing. It was a crazy and exciting time. To help with learning, we created a library at each office, where anyone could take a book to read or give a book to someone they felt it might help. The company would normally keep three to five copies of a book on hand, and reorder as needed.

Learning at the IRCE show in Chicago

Special Star from the IT Dept

We started RT University, where folks could learn more for both hard and soft skills. This was an education platform where you would answer a number of questions. Based on your feedback, it would show where you were strong and where you

Learn More Earn More progress chart

were not so strong. It then offered things you could do to enhance your skills, whether it was a book to read, video to watch, or an exercise to do. It could be customized for the entire company, a department, or an individual. You could then track your progress.

It offered skill training to enhance for your job at RealTruck, such as order processing, but it would also have other skills such as speaking, how to lead a meeting or design a Powerpoint. RealTruck basic training and the "Learn more, Earn more," which included customer service, returns, and order fulfillment training, was moved into it. Since most of the university was self-led, other than the basics and learn more earn more, it never fully got embraced by the culture. With some of the advanced training, it was always a challenge to come up with a good answer as to how much time at work someone could use to partake in the platform. In retrospect, we should have recruited a professor type to lead the training like we did for the basic and LMEM training.

In our HR department we changed almost everything, from our job application, how we wrote job posting ads and descriptions, to our interview process and more. We also changed our employee evaluations, our handbook and more.

The best kind of MD to get— "To an awesome customer service rep! Have a great day!"

All of it centered around delivering more, transparency, improve, take risks, include fun and be humble.

Our job descriptions were written transparently, included fun, and were always evolving. The same was true of our job ads. We asked ourselves, what could we do to deliver more, be transparent, improve, and include fun to people applying for a job with us? We wanted to hire for culture fit first and skills second. We knew having someone who was really skilled but wasn't a culture fit would be bad in the long run, so it was important we hired great culture fits first. That started with transparent and fun job ads and descriptions. Our job ads were so funny that sometimes folks would write us to thank us for a good laugh while job hunting. Others would share them socially or even post them up on forums praising us for best job ad ever. We all know that job hunting is usually not very enjoyable, so our goal was to attract the right people and to also make people's day who were job hunting.

Here are what a few of the smaller sample ads might look like:

> *Want more fun at work? Do you look good wearing a superhero cape? Bottomless coffee, no-dress code and endless potlucks. Check out RealTruck.com/Careers*

> *Do you have mad super-hero skills? Always wanting to save the day. Do you find yourself going to any length to make a customer or fellow employee smile? All the sweet bennys like bottomless coffee, snacks and even Don Johnson dress up days.*
> *RealTruck.com/Careers*

Best Job Post Ever posted on a forum

Here is an example of a web job description:

Lead Web Developer Wanted (with or without cape)

About RealTruck

As a 2013 North Dakota Young Professionals Network Best Places to Work runner-up, we put our Guiding Principles into practice to create a unique, fun, and rewarding work environment. We are a leading online retailer of pickup truck accessories and the 14th fastest-growing e-commerce site nationwide on a mission to make people's lives and vehicles better.

Your Backstory (Job Summary):

You're a web programmer who has been searching the 4 corners of the earth for the perfect, little, sleepy, town to hang your hat and call home. You've been fighting mighty bugs and code demons for an eternity and you're ready to face your most daunting challenge yet. This quest moves fast, has numerous hidden traps and will take you down pitch black caverns and straight over the most rugged mountains. You've been preparing for this quest all your life. You are ready. Now is the time. (This translates to: We're looking to add a full-time Lead Web Developer to our team, located in Fargo, ND with a starting salary of $XX/year).[9] Take a glimpse at what your future job could be. https://www.youtube.com/X

A Hero's Attributes (Requirements):
- *5+ years experience in HTML, Javascript, PHP, SQL*
- *2+ years experience in git and Linux*
- *In-depth knowledge of design patterns and use them often*
- *Knowledge of modern programming practices*
- *Previous experience of managing a team of 3 or more.*
- *Uncanny attention to detail*
- *Previous experience modernizing legacy code*
- *Must be able to stay focused and organized in a fast paced company*
- *Must have a burning passion to improve and continue learning*
- *Strong leadership qualities and the ability to challenge the status quo*

---

9   This an old job description. The links, $ and % amounts have been replaced by a XX.

Your Quest (Responsibilities):
- *Lead technical discussions and push emerging technologies*
- *Lead detailed architectural planning discussions*
- *Pull request reviews*
- *Conduct code reviews or other team learning events*
- *Help the dev team grow through coaching*
- *Speak your mind freely and have respectful passionate debates*
- *Keep pushing internal refactoring projects forward while balancing regular feature requests*
- *Be a great communicator! Take leave from battling the mighty dragon and be able to explain very complex and abstract concepts to others without them running in fear*
- *Work hard, have fun, and be a part of something great!*

Bonus Skills:
- *Lucene, Solr or Elasticsearch experience. (+5 Charisma)*
- *Hands on experience using Symfony or Silex (+5 Robot Overlord)*
- *RabbitMQ experience (+10 Agility)*

You saved the princess! (Benefits):[10]
RealTruck offers benefits to all full-time employees in accordance with the employee handbook including, but not limited to:

What we think you need:
- *Health, dental and vision coverage*
- *401K with up to X% company match*
- *Company-paid Life Insurance*
- *Paid Time Off (Up to X days your first year)*
- *X Holidays off*

What we think you want:
- *Profit Sharing*
- *Bottomless Coffee*
- *Free Birthday Lunch*
- *Tons of Delicious Potlucks*
- *No Dress Code*
- *Employee Discount*

---

10   These benefits were from 2015 and may no longer apply.

CHAPTER 6

Example IT Help Desk position

We're doing cool stuff in North Dakota: "2006, RealTruck.Com received an Innovation Award from the Information Technology Council of North Dakota." RealTruck.com has been innovating web technology for more than a decade. (Yup, we've been around since Al Gore invented the internet) First established in 1998 from a basement apartment, we've grown in to a leading retailer of automotive accessories and automotive lifestyle products. Our Guiding Principles shape who we are and how we operate.

Summary
We're looking for a helpful and friendly addition to our IT team to help support our growing Jamestown office. We have a few dozen machines that need some TLC and we need an outgoing problem solver to kick some 0x436f6d707574465722041 7373

Requirements
- *Support Windows 7, Windows Server a plus*
- *Must enjoy that "New Computer Smell"*
- *Support MS Office 2007+ products*
- *Must be a Fan of "The IT Crowd"*
- *Support Google Apps*
- *Able to adapt to new technologies*
- *Must bathe daily*

Responsibilities
- *Resolve Computer Support Issues*
- *Setup and maintain workstations and peripherals*
- *Respond to tech help requests from local and remote staff*
- *Must quote Darth Vader often*
- *Maintain machine security compliance*
- *Organize and maintain IT assets*
- *Deliver More by proactively seeking out support issues with staff*
- *Setup and configure IPhone and Droid devices*

- *Maintain Records and Processes*
- *Log issues to simple task system for follow up and visibility*
- *Document current procedures and assets*
- *Actively recommend enhancements to current processes*
- *Ongoing Technology Training*
- *Support future VOIP system*
- *Create training videos for the rest of the RealTruck crew*
- *Embrace opportunities to help others learn more about technology through 1:1 communication or presentations*

Benefits

This will be a full time, salaried position. Starting pay varies between XX and XX DOE. RealTruck, Inc. offers comprehensive benefits to all full-time employees in accordance with probationary periods and employee handbook including, but not limited to:

- *Health, Dental and Vision Coverage*
- *An absurd number of Pot Luck Lunches*
- *401 (k)*
- *Life Insurance*
- *Asbestos Free Environment*
- *Bottomless Coffee*
- *Paid Vacation*
- *Ability to wear a superhero cape without anyone thinking twice*
- *Holiday Pay*

HIRE CHARACTER FIRST

The first interview was done to determine if there was a culture and principle fit. Initially this was done by the hiring manager and HR. Over time it would be conducted by members of the culture team, which consisted of two or three people. They would be interviewed with questions around our guiding principles. If they understood them and were able to share examples of practicing them in their everyday life, then they would be called back for a skill interview with the hiring manager and a few members of the team. It made the process longer, but we hired better. Like everything else, these things were always evolving. Jeff Vanlaningham and Lucy Geigle were often the ones leading the charge on the questions and processes. As we asked ourselves more questions—why are we asking these questions? what are we looking for?—the questions we asked candidates and the entire new hire process got better. If we wanted to bring someone in for an interview, we also tried to give them a pretty good heads-up of what to expect for the first interview.

We also wanted to try to deliver more to them and make them as related as possible. If someone is overly nervous in an interview, it's hard to really get a feel for who they are. So they might be surprised with someone in a bear costume or a gift for visiting us. We might even start the interview with asking who their favorite Star Wars character is or asking what was the nicest thing someone did for them recently. We wanted them to really experience our culture, even in the interview process. Our culture questions were about trying to see if they could see and identify the guiding principle in other people's actions and their personal experience on practicing them. Here are two examples showing the evolution of the process:

Example Initial Culture Fit Questions

DELIVER MORE

1. Can you share a couple examples when someone really pleasantly wowed you?
2. Can you share some examples of when you really went out of your way to help someone?
3. When was the last time your pleasantly surprised someone? What did you do?
4. What is the best customer service you have ever experienced?

TRANSPARENCY ROCKS

1. Describe a time you had to have a candid and frank conversation with someone.
2. Have you ever asked your boss or coworkers what you could do to be a better employee? What did they say?
3. Share a couple of things you would like the world to know about you.
4. Share a time you asked for help with something.
5. What is something you would like to get better at?

IMPROVE

1. What is something new you have recently learned personally or professionally?
2. Share a time you changed something.
3. What was the last book, video, or article you learned something from? What was it?
4. The last time someone changed something you didn't like, what did you do?
5. Share a time you changed your opinion about something.

Take Risks

1. Share a time you tried something and it failed.
2. Share a time you took a risk and it turned out well.
3. What is one of the biggest risks you ever took?
4. Share a time you changed something without asking for permission.

Include Fun

1. Share something in the past week or two that you did that was fun.
2. Share a time you went out of your way to add a little fun to something.
3. What are a few fun things you would like to do in the future?
4. What is the funniest thing you ever did at work?

Be Humble

1. Share a time you went out of your way to compliment someone.
2. What is something you did that made it better for the next person?
3. At your last job, were you ever asked to do something you felt was beneath you to do? What did you do?
4. Share a time you took responsibility for something that failed or didn't work out as you had hoped.
5. Share a time you passed on credit to someone for their contribution, even though you did more of the work.

These answers were rated on a scale of 1 to 5 by the interviewers. If the combined ratings were 3.5 or higher, they would be called back for a skill set interviewer. Like everything else, these questions and processes were always evolving. Here is an example of the evolution to more of a pass or fail rating system:

Evolution of Culture Fit Questions

First Questions: (Open Response)
- What was it about RealTruck that attracted you to apply?
- How did you hear about RealTruck and the position you applied for?

Guiding Principle Questions: (Pass/Fail and response)

- What is something you have done at work that you are proud of?

  Pass: Have a good example and a story that backs that up.

  Fail: They haven't done anything at work that they are proud of, not a good example and not grasping the idea of deliver more.

- How do you handle a situation where you feel that your opinion was not heard at work?

  Pass: Address the situation by talking with the person in a setting that is appropriate, explain your side and be willing to hear their side. Come to an agreed upon understanding.

  Fail: Make a big deal about it, confront the individual in a situation that would be inappropriate to have a conversation, hold a grudge over the situation, be spiteful of that individual in future situations. Not saying anything at all.

- Describe the last time you went out of your way to do something for another person, and how did it make you feel? (Make sure they explain how it made them feel)

  Pass: have an example and don't struggle to find a situation to talk about. Personal or professional.

  Fail: Has a hard time coming up with an example.

- Have you encountered miscommunication at your last/current job? How did you handle it?

  Pass: define the struggle, speaking on the resolution. Talk about how they prevent it from happening again.

  Fail: Never had miscommunication, blame the other person, no ownership of the issue. Not listening to others point. Not addressing the situation.

- When was the last time you asked for help? Did you get the help you needed?

  Pass: Example that resonates. Able to admit that they need help. Able to learn, to prevent asking for help over and over.

  Fail: Never asking for help. They didn't get the help and blame others.

- Give us an example of a time where you pushed for change in your current/previous position.

  Pass: Example and how it impacted the company. Could be a situation where they tried and failed. Honesty.

  Fail: No example. No initiative to try again.

- What is a mistake you have made that taught you a valuable lesson?

  Pass: Gives an example and is sincere about learning from the situation

  Fail: doesn't make mistakes, not sincere about learning from a mistake, or gives a poor example and explanation.

- How do you adjust to a change that you don't agree with?

  Pass: Embrace it and try to work around your feelings about the change. Push back but willing to adapt.

  Fail: Unwilling to adjust.

- What's a risk you've taken in your life that has paid off big time?

  Pass: Explains a situation and why it was a risk. (looking for sincerity)

  Fail: Explains a situation that really isn't a risk and does not offer a lot of explanation and is not sincere.

- What do you do when you disagree with your manager?

  Pass: Have a conversation about the situation, come to an understanding and move forward. Come to a compromise about the situation. Understanding of where each party is coming from.

  Fail: Confront the manager about the situation to argue why they are wrong. Escalate the situation more. Spiteful in their actions.

- How do you turn Monday into a day you look forward to?

  Pass: attitude, positivity, things and stuff

  Fail: Monday is crap.

- Name 3 characteristics of being a humble person?

  Pass: Is able to give 3 characteristics and defend why they choose them. Must be part of being humble and not just 3 random characteristics.

  Fail: Unable to come up with anything, Can't explain why they choose them. Chooses 3 that have nothing to do with being humble.

Final Questions: (Open Response)
- Why would you be a good fit for RealTruck's Culture?
- What is most important to you in your next job?

This last pass or fail example was also used along the way because of feedback suggesting that in a 1-5 scale, it was more difficult to be consistent from one interviewer to the next and a pass or fail rating would be easier to rate. This point is to show willingness to try something different. Measure the results and adjust from there.

About technology. This was an area that experienced incredible improvement. Because the web development and IT departments were getting copied on the questions and answers from other departments and participating in basics training along with actively supporting the customer service team during the busy holiday season, they became more aware of the problems they needed to find solutions for.

Sometimes, for something that was a huge obstacle for the customer service team, a solution could be developed with an hour of code writing. For example, a common problem in customer service was a customer would call and ask about the costs and shipping times on a few parts. They would say they needed to chat with their significant other and would call us back. Sometimes in five minutes and other times in five days. On the second call, the customer service rep would have to re-enter the year, make, and model of the vehicle, re-find the parts the customer was interested in and place the order.

The development team in short order came up with a solution. They added a save the cart function to the website. The customer or the customer service rep could quickly click a button to save that cart and enter the email address of the customer. It would email the customer the cart along with a reference number. The customer could either check out on their own or if they called back, the customer service rep could quickly pull up the cart. This took the development team about an hour of coding. The time cost savings alone was huge along with the convenience it created for the customer.

So if we received a hundred calls a day and it took on average four minutes to add the vehicle info and find the parts, and this save the cart tool now allowed you to do it in ten seconds, the time savings alone in a year was over 2,000 hours.

This kind of thing was happening across all departments. One of the cooler things we did was what we called our Auto-PO-Bot. Since we were a drop ship company, that meant if you were the order fulfillment department (OFS), for every order that came in, at least one or more purchase orders (PO) needed to be created and sent to a vendor. That PO would need to be confirmed by the vendor and shipped out.

The tracking needed to be relayed back to us and posted in the system to notify the customer the item shipped. Then the PO had to be changed in the accounting system from open to fulfilled so it could be matched up with the invoice from the vendor. This department ran with only a few people when sales were $60 million. Let me break it down a little. $60 million in sales means about 360,000 purchase orders a year, about 7,000 a week, or about 1,375 a day in a five-day work week. That also means 1,375 order confirmations, 1,375 tracking numbers and 1,375 completed POs per day. How could only three or four people possibly do that? Short answer is by managing the exception rather than the rule.

The first thing we needed to do was make sure that we never sold anything that couldn't be shipped and that we never sent a PO to a vendor that didn't have the part in stock. If we did that, then we would have to go through the work of cancelling the PO and reissuing it to a vendor that did have it in stock.

To do this, development worked with our partners to get inventory feeds on what they had in stock and what they didn't have in stock. For most parts, we got them directly from the manufacturer, but we also had relationships with wholesale distributors for the same parts. We got inventory feeds from both. If no one had the part in stock, it would be turned off on the website so folks couldn't order it. We could set the purchasing order. So for part X, order from the manufacturer first; if not in stock then try warehouse distributor 1, warehouse distributor 2, and so forth. When the customer's order came in, our Auto-PO-Bot would process it and send it to the best vendor and automatically post it to the accounting system.

We would get confirmation back when the PO was received so the OFS team didn't need to manually follow up on it. Once the vendor shipped, we would get tracking and that would automatically post to the order to notify the customer and into the accounting system to complete the PO. Since we knew if the vendor had it in stock and also knew historically how fast a vendor shipped something out, we only had to manually follow up with POs that were outside of this time frame. Yes, I loved that little Auto-PO-Bot.

This also helped our partners. Often a partner might think that if they had something in stock, it shipped the same day. Because we shared data with our partners, we could let them know if this was true or not.

One of our partners thought that if we got them a PO before 1pm, it would ship the same day. Our data said this was not true. It was taking up to five days for the item to ship after we sent the PO in. We shared this data with the partner. What the partner discovered was that if their warehouse got the order by 1pm, it shipped out the same day. The problem was, they weren't getting all the orders the same day they came in. Our partner's customer service team was five days behind on entering orders into their system. With this information, the vendor was able to come up with a better solution to get orders they received into their system in real time.

Marketing fully engaged with this principle as well. Being a drop ship company from North Dakota, you have to be good at marketing. Especially since less than 1% of our sales came from North Dakota. In the spirit of transparency and a desire to improve, we reached out to our advertising partners at Google, Bing, YouTube, and so forth to set up regular training meetings with them via Google Hangouts or Skype.

We expanded this practice to a great deal of our third-party software partners as well, so we could get the most out of their tools. We attended national trade shows like IRCE (Internet Retailers Conference and Exhibition) and

CHAPTER 6

SMX (Search Marketing Expo) so we could increase our learning from the bigger e-commerce companies from around the country and gain insights into e-commerce and marketing best practices. The reality is that most folks, if you ask, want to help you. The first step is asking.

Our videos also began to evolve around helping customers. We did what we called fast facts videos, which were ideally under 60 seconds on what someone at RealTruck liked about a product. These were posted on various video platforms and also added to the website. These videos were just real people sharing real thoughts. We also started doing product installation videos along with videos sharing our culture, how-to videos, and fun videos like including fun at the SEMA show.

People often ask me, how do you get 25,000,000 channel views on YouTube? The simple answer is just post eight helpful videos a week. Often companies try to swing for the fence and try to create a viral video. They post a video or two they think is viral material. It gets 500 views and flames out. Two, three, or six months later, they try another grand video production and again get the same result. Our thoughts were, it's really hard to create a viral video. Not that we shouldn't try, but we should regularly post genuine videos, with genuine people.

These regularly posted videos shouldn't be overly scripted, they should embrace our guiding principles, and they shouldn't be trying to compete with the skills of a Coca-Cola commercial. Yes, we should take the time and resources and try to do those kind of videos, but not as the replacement for posting helpful videos regularly. It also helps if you take the time to organize and make the video titles and descriptions user and search engine friendly, along with putting videos in appropriate playlists that are also user and search engine friendly.

Last, watching folks engage and share their adventures with personal learning and growth was very rewarding, along with people throughout the company praising them for it. Everything from someone learning a new language or how to juggle to going to college or learning how to dance. It was fun to watch people also take the time to pass on to others something they learned. Sometimes folks would set up a class to pass on what they learned to anyone who wanted to sign up, from photography to how to use a cool phone app or music lessons and beer brewing.

This quote sums up this principle:

> *"How wonderful it is that nobody need wait a single moment before starting to improve the world."*
> —Anne Frank

Entry way at the Jamestown office

Improve poster

Jeff doing some coaching with the crew

Meeting area of the Fargo office

Someone working too hard (having a little fun on Halloween)

Sleeve tattoo day; can you guess the "real" one?

7
TAKE RISKS

"Babe Ruth was not afraid to strike out.
And it was this fearlessness that contributed
to his remarkable career."
—Simon Sinek

Don't be afraid to take risks. Leadership doesn't come from authority, rather the ability to help others achieve more than they thought they could. You have the authority and power to take risks and make mistakes. It is ok to make mistakes, provided we learn from them. Don't accept status quo or that's how we've always done it. We should be adventurous and always be striving to make something better. We want to be creative and unconventional with our solutions. An entrepreneurial spirit and taking risks is needed and is what allows us the possibility of being exceptional.

4. Take Risks

B eing such a natural risk taker, I'm often surprised by how paralyzed some folks become when taking a risk, making a decision, or wanting to point elsewhere for the reason something was done or not done. When it comes to success, the credit takers are easy to find.

Take Risks can be a tough guiding principle for many of us. We wanted to remove this fear and empower anyone to take risks. Sometimes we will fail and then learn from it. Take Risks—This was probably one of our most challenging

GPs in the sense that we did a lot to encourage people to task risks, but still had challenges to ensure people didn't feel threatened or penalized for taking a risk. We also needed to tune it so the risks were calculated ones. Having an entire culture of people calling this out when we saw a person or a team doing it certainly helped getting folks to take more risks. This is ultimately the biggest driver for creating change and killing status quo.

WHAT PREVENTS US FROM TAKING RISKS?

When we rolled this out, we started with questions.
- What are some times that not taking a risk may hurt me?
- When are some times that not taking a risk may hurt RealTruck?
- If I could change three things at RealTruck, what would they be?
- What is stopping me from making those changes?
- What are 3 things our team could do better?
- What can I do to help my team do those three things better?

As various teams and departments met, we obtained answers, identified obstacles, and began to take actions. The RealTruck pins, bracelets, and buttons, along with the company-wide shout outs, really helped bring this principle to reality in the culture.

Some of the concerns of taking risks include:
- Getting in trouble
- Losing job
- Looking bad
- Failure

Some of the rewards of taking risks include:
- Being a hero
- Getting promoted
- Looking good
- Success

The challenge here was learning where we needed to reduce the fears and increase awareness of the rewards. This was our course. If someone took a risk and it didn't work out or failed altogether, as a company we would praise them for taking the risk in the first place. As for getting in trouble— yes, someone may talk with you about it, a leader or manager, but that doesn't mean you are in trouble. Rather, checking to see what you learned from the experience and to pass on any tips they might have for you in the future.

As for the fear of losing your job, at RealTruck we tried to convey that wouldn't happen from practicing the guiding principles. As for looking bad, we tried to emphasize no risk, no reward. Yes, taking a calculated risk may go sideways on you, but sometimes that is how we learn. Learn from it and move on. Realize you may look bad temporarily, but the experience gained will benefit you moving forward. Failure too is temporary. Often, the home run king or queen for a team is also the strikeout king or queen. We have to get up and keep swinging the bat. Calling out when someone took a risk, the results good or bad, learning lessons, and rewards propelled this into our culture.

Having fun with postcards

WHY TAKE RISKS?

> **"***The biggest risk is not taking any risk...***
> ***In a world that's changing really quickly,***
> ***the only strategy that is guaranteed to fail is not taking risks.***"
> —*Mark Zuckerberg*

We really pushed the idea that if you take a risk and succeed, you will be happy. If you fail, you will be wise.

TAKE RISKS = HAPPY OR WISE

We had to get everyone on board that it was okay to take risks and you have permission to do so because of this guiding principle. Slowly and sometimes quickly, we began to see results in the company wide realization that not making a decision, which often involves taking a risk, is a decision to be status quo.

I've never been a big fan of job titles. In those early days, if I had to give a title, it would just be that I worked at RealTruck. However, when dealing with outside partners, it was hard to get by company gatekeepers, with the title of "I just work at RealTruck." I started to describe myself as the self-appointed CEO or the CEO in training. I suppose there was always a part of me that felt, if we had to pick a CEO, it probably wouldn't have been me. I never liked the title of Human Resource Manager. I'm not sure exactly why, except that I didn't really care for the idea of looking at people as just a resource or something you just use. They are people. I was very happy with our Human Resource Manager, Lucy Geigle, so I took a risk and changed her title to Chief People Officer. I thought that better described what she did and was reflective of our culture. Debi, our Customer Service Manager, followed suit and became the Director of Happiness.

The Deliver More, Transparency, Improve, Include Fun, and Be Humble principles all require risk taking. In customer service, I started to hear folks answer the phones with a little of their personality. One of my favorites was from

Real Peeps having fun

Meet the team postcards

Johnny Jerome and it went something like, "Thanks for calling RealTruck.com, this is Johnny. We make dreams come true. How can I help you?" At the end of the call, he would close with something like, "Thanks for calling RealTruck.com. Is there anything else I can do to make your life or your vehicle better?" Some of the answers he received gave him more opportunities to deliver more.

Next thing you know, Customer Service was sending personal thank you cards to customers. Some were self-created and others were your basic thank you card with a personalized message inside. Marketing noticed this and created some interesting thank you and meet the team postcards. Over time, the goal became to get some kind of customer serendipity to 10% of our customers. This might include a thank you postcard, courtesy phone call, or some of our more interesting swag gifts like fuzzy dice and over the top T-shirts. Two of my favorite shirts included "If looking good is a crime, my ride is doing time" and "I like big trucks and I cannot lie." Debi Reberg, our Director of Happiness, started cutting out and putting customer comments on the wall. This expanded to more walls and into the staircases.

As people in the customer service department took smaller risks, their ability to take bigger calculated risks began. Whether it was a new team being created to modernize and make our customer service policies more reflective of our guiding principles, or someone stepping up and creating a proposal for why we needed a new telephone system, which one we should buy, and requesting to pitch it to upper management. And when the leadership team said do it, they did and reported on the results.

Development took it upon themselves to hang up "It's OK to…" and "published is better than perfect" posters around the office. This was good for transparency and a good visual reminder that it's okay to take risks and fail. As for the "published is better than perfect" posters, it was a great message for speeding up development. Plus, they were probably tired of hearing my un-signed million dollar check story.

This was something I shared: it may feel good to have a million dollar check in your pocket, but if it's not signed, it's worthless. Nobody gets any benefit from something almost done. Having something 95% complete doesn't get us any return on our invested time or resources. In web development or any other department, it's easy to have 25 things almost done, but in reality that's a lot of work and effort that no one is getting any return on.

Clearly we didn't want poor development or average execution; however, we did need to knock down barriers that got in the way of something getting done as quickly as possible, and in the case of web development, publish what

we can, as fast as we can. If we were developing a new product layout that included how we were displaying the images and product features, if we had the product features completed, we could publish that, rather than waiting for the image display portion to be finished and doing one big publish.

Shooting a pic for a new postcard

Happy Holidays with Santa Jeff

If the image display took a month longer, then we would not get the benefit of the better product features as soon as we could.

Another example would be if we were updating the product recommendation tool across the site. It affects a number of page types including category pages, vehicle pages, brand pages, product line pages, part pages, and the home page. Rather than doing all the coding for all the pages and doing one massive publish, the development team evolved to publish each area as it was completed. Rather than waiting six months for one big publish, we got smaller enhanced publishes every couple of weeks.

Development also began taking a more active role in guiding stakeholders that were requesting new features and technology. If someone in marketing requested a new feature for the website, development would really dig in to find out the real need and real benefit we were trying to accomplish, balance that with what technology was available and what would most likely be the best long term solution. In the past, they would just develop whatever was requested, and if it involved a third party tool, integrate with whomever was requested. Now, they were digging in and discovering the real needs. They would do some research and often come back with a better solution or a better third party to integrate with.

Marketing wanted to have some automated emails going out to past customers recommending products they might like. Marketing learned of a third party provider we will call "DoMore," an email company that offered this automation, and the cost would easily be paid for by the increase in sales. Marketing could update the template anytime and the emails could auto-populate products the customer might like based on any data we provided.

Marketing was sure they had everything we needed. Development dug in and found out what marketing really needed and also dug into what the provider really could do and not do. Marketing wanted automated emails that went out two weeks after someone placed an order, and they wanted to be able to update the template from time to time to recommended popular products that specifically fit that customer's exact vehicle, and to exclude the category of product they had previously purchased.

What development had discovered was that "DoMore" email company was more expensive than the average email marketing company. They also discovered that while they could automatically populate popular products, they could not do it factoring in the type of vehicle the customer owned, but they were working on it and would most likely have it in short order. Development also discovered that there were not any user tools for someone in marketing to be able to update the template. The templates could only be updated by the provider. Development was experienced enough to know that there are lots of third party software companies sales staff that tended to over-promise what the software could actually do.

Let's Break Something poster

Had development just done what marketing initially requested, we would have been in a one year contract with a company that didn't really provide the solution we were seeking. Our product recommendations might fit the vehicle the customer owned and the template could be updated, but it was a manual process that could take a week or so. What development did find, after some research, was another provider that could do everything we needed and more. Some of the additional features not only included popular products for the vehicle the customer owned, but also factored in popular products often bought with the products they already owned along with taking into account the geographical popularity of a product. And the bonus was, this company offered more for less money.

WHAT IF TAKING A RISK FAILS?

There was failure too, which is where we learned the most. In HR, to try to include some fun, someone had the idea to add about 15 *Star Wars* movie questions to the interview process with no real idea why they were asking the questions in the first place. Going back to always asking why we are doing something helps weed out the things we shouldn't be doing. If you understand *Star Wars*, it was probably pretty fun; if you didn't, you probably left thinking what a bunch of weirdos.

A brand manager had the idea that if we could sell pickup accessories, maybe we could also sell 12-volt type products, oils, and farm-related products; even some dog food from Cenex got loaded to the site at one time. Since dog food didn't really fit into our mission, along with having the company name of RealTruck, it was removed.

But this got us asking questions. Like, why are we loading car part data? After doing some digging, we discovered 40% of our data was for cars. Car accessories represented less than 1% of our sales. We needed to accept the brutal fact that even though a lot of our customers might own cars, they weren't getting their car accessories from us. So when someone in the brands department was adding a new product, 40% of their application data work was for 1% of our sales. The other 60% represented 99% of our sales.

The original theory was, when we were adding a product, looking at it one product at a time, also adding the car data seemed easy enough to do and wasn't that much more work. The reality is that it was 40% more work for only 1% of our sales. Someone in the brands team came up with a plan to start removing car data from the website. First they started with the year, make, and model of cars we had never sold anything for. Over time we virtually had no car data. Removing the car data naturally reduced the work for loading new products and maintaining existing products, and it actually helped increase sales because our pickup customers could select their specific year, make, and model faster and see all the products that fit their vehicle faster. This is another example of how the "stop doing" list can not only save you time, but greatly enhance your business and overall sales. We were helping our primary customers, pickup owners, find parts for their truck faster and easier.

Dream space walls were created in which a person could hang up a picture and the name of something they were dreaming about getting or accomplishing. This was great for really knowing some folks' wildest dreams. As you accomplished it, you would replace it with another dream. Some of the items on the dream space walls were more conservative, such as going to college, and others a little more wild, like going to space. In any case, it helped us connect with each other better.

WHAT ABOUT MARKETING?

As for our marketing department, this guiding principle was a blank check for them. It started with small things like how HR announced that since we were getting bigger, visitors would need to sign in and wear a visitor badge. Marketing took a risk and created some very interesting visitor badges. They gave the visitor a laugh, and were so funny you didn't mind wearing one even if you weren't a visitor. My favorite was the one that said visitor along with "I'm not saying I'm Batman, I'm just saying no one has ever seen Batman and I in the same room together."

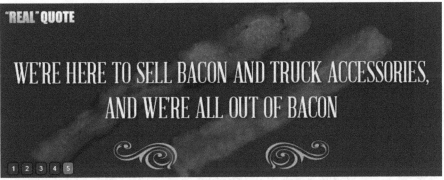

Website front page banner

I have to say, one day I pulled up the website and the main home banner said, "We sell bacon and truck accessories, and we're all out of bacon." I about choked on my coffee laughing so hard. I loved it. Our culture was evolving.

When YouTube ads and Facebook ads started coming out, the team cut the budget from our traditional keyword ads on Bing and Google and started testing ads on these new platforms. They just took a risk and did it and reported the results. What this did was allow us to learn how to optimize those advertising platforms quickly and in some cases years ahead of our competitors.

And in the digital and e-commerce worlds, mastering a new marketing area or platform and really dialing it in for effective return on ads spend, as fast as possible, can put you ahead of the competition for years to come.

If you are not familiar with e-commerce, one big difference between traditional marketing and e-commerce marketing is how you budget. A traditional business might have a fixed advertising budget; in the digital e-commerce world, you don't have a fixed budget, as that would not be timely enough, nor realistic for the data and analytics an e-commerce company has access to. For digital ads, when you can track sales and conversions with great detail, the budget becomes more of a math equation; it depends on the product and category, and what the margin is for that product or category you are selling online. Based on that, you can figure out what you can spend to get a sale. So the budget becomes, if the return on ad spend (ROAS) is equal to or greater than X, turn up the ad spend. Spend as much as you can, provided you keep in the acceptable ROAS range.

Here's an example.

Equation: Revenue divided by ad spend = Return On Ad Spend (ROAS)

Assume your ad spend = $100 and that created $1,000 in revenue. That would make the Return On Ad Spend = 10. If your product margin is 30% then $100 in ad spend gives you $300 in margin. Less the $100 in ad cost spent gives you $200 in margin left. To boil it down, if your ROAS is 10, every $100 in ad spend gives you $200 in margin. Technically, the ROAS could even drop to as low as 4, and at 30% margin, you would still be keeping a positive margin, although it wouldn't be much. With a product with 30% margin, the minimum

Deliver More Cards Awesome

Deliver More Cards Awesome--inside

RT holiday party fun

Making some creative videos at the SEMA Show

acceptable ROAS I might recommend would be around 5 to 8 depending on the overhead. If you can get a 10 to 1 ROAS, then my question to you is, what are you waiting for? TURN IT UP.

The last story to share is about building a truck. The truck of all trucks. The marketing team decided to take a huge risk and build a custom truck. We would do this with the help of our partners and take it to the SEMA show. We would video building it and post the progress from start to finish. In addition, we would create fast fact product videos along with installation videos of each of the products installed. Initially, it was going to be a StormTrooper truck. A truck that a StormTrooper from *Star Wars* would want to drive. It would be all white with a few slight black accents. The marketing team took off running with the idea. Next thing you know, we have a team created to build it, comprised of both internal and external resources, and partners were shipping products to us left and right for the truck build.

The initial response was great. Then we realized, we probably needed permission to build a StormTrooper truck from *Star Wars* and Lucas Films. It's one thing for someone to personally customize their truck and paint a Superman logo on it. It's quite another thing for a business to do this. We tried everything we could to get permission, but at that time, no one was getting permission to license anything from *Star Wars*, and certainly some little company from North Dakota probably wasn't going to be the first test case for a truck build.

Another risk was taken and the new name of the truck became the Storm Truck. The Storm Truck project was

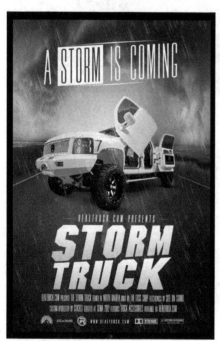

Storm Truck movie poster

an example of Taking Risks, Delivering More, Including Fun, and of course Improve since we had never done anything quite like this. Jim and his two sons at the Foss Shop in Casselton, ND, did all the painting and customization. Butch and his crew at Site On Sound in Fargo, ND, did all the LED lighting, TVs, electronics, sound system and, to our knowledge, the first-ever iPad used to control all the gadgets in the truck. Our marketing and video team did all the videos, posters and various marketing materials on the truck.

This jacked up pickup had everything from a barn door tailgate with TVs along with a great big flat screen TV that rose up when you opened the truck

Building the Storm Truck at The Foss Shop

At the Sema Show with the Storm Truck

bed cover, to Lambo front doors, suicide back doors and a full customized interior with cool blue LED lighting. To top it off, you could play an Xbox inside or outside the truck. We figured out how to get it to Vegas and displayed it at the SEMA show in the Light Truck Accessory Alliance (LTAA) industry booth for all to see. It was an awesome experience.

We did go over budget a little too much and learned a bunch along the way. The general concept continued, except now we were much better at sticking to the budget. Some of the more memorable truck builds included a Beauty vs. Beast build and Big Red build. Beauty vs. Beast was where we customized two identical Ford F150 trucks, one that was styled for the street and the other all jacked up and styled for the off-road. Big Red was a red GMC truck we jacked up with a lift kit and big wheels along with all the standard truck goodies like a bed cover, bed liner, and some trick LED lighting.

THE REWARD

One of the greatest rewards of watching this principle get into the culture was that it really gave us the ability to change quickly, find better solutions faster, and it was the spark that enabled us to do many things we didn't think we could do. And doing better than you thought you would is always a real blessing.

...

4. Take Risks

Take Risks poster

The Big Red Truck project

Beauty vs Beast trucks project

Thank you to everyone involved with building the Storm Truck.
Your hard work and dedication to the project was truly inspiring.

8
INCLUDE FUN

*"People rarely succeed unless they have fun
in what they are doing."*
—Dale Carnegie

Don't just have fun, create it. We want RealTruck to be an enjoyable and memorable experience for our customers, partners and each other. In our pursuit of happiness, we want to add fun and excitement to all areas of our company. From how we design our web pages, conduct meetings to our interaction with people, we strive to practice our guiding principles. We believe the happier and more enjoyable we are the more productive we can be. Always remembering, that we take our responsibilities serious, but not ourselves.

5. Include Fun

W e spent a lot of time at work. If we were going to spend that much time somewhere, we figured that we owed it to ourselves and those around us to have some fun along the way. It only takes a minute or two to add fun to a meeting, an email, a web page, our office, our work area, our break room, a meeting with a vendor, phone call to a customer, or whatever comes up during the day.

This was probably the best guiding principle we were known for. All of

Visitor badges

Fargo office doing a dance video

Marketing having fun on April Fool's Day

them were important, and this simple idea made everything a little more enjoyable. Fun creates memorable experiences, which are good for the soul and even good for marketing, as the fun that was created for customers and business partners made RealTruck very memorable. These positive and memorable experiences helped keep customers coming back and even inspired some of them to join in and create their own fun with us.

This guiding principle was rolled out just like the other ones; we focused on it for two months to get it better ingrained into everything we were doing. This was one of the easier principles for folks to get their minds, hearts, and actions around. Now clearly, everyone's definition of acceptable fun varied. There's the screwing-off kind of fun and there's the have a little fun as you're working. This principle was about including fun. Certainly, there is a need to have the screwing-off kind of fun from time to time. But including fun while we are working is something we could try to incorporate in everything. Some folks are better at creating fun than others, just like some principles are easier for some to practice than others. However, all of us can choose or not choose to participate in fun when it's going on around us.

Not everyone who goes to a concert is screaming and hollering. Some are really into the concert big time. Others are just there, not really getting into the music, and there are a few scowling in disapproval. If you are going to go to an AC/DC concert, you need to have the right attitude. That kind of music and concert doesn't fit everyone. That doesn't mean they have bad taste in music; they might have great musical taste, it's just not a good fit for them. RealTruck was no different. It wasn't for everyone. Back then at RealTruck, if you weren't cool with a floor full of people clapping and cheering when someone came into the building, RealTruck probably wouldn't be a good fit for you.

UPS ad circulated around office for a little fun

For the rollout we started with questions and started getting feedback from everyone in the company.

1. Where are we not including fun with customers?
2. Where are we not including fun with partners?
3. Where are we not including fun with each other?
4. What can we do to add a little fun for customers?
5. What can we do to add a little fun for partners?
6. What can we do to add a little fun for each other?
7. What can the company do to help us be able to include fun in everything we do?

The answers that came back were different from one department to another. It was very clear that we had lots of opportunities to add fun to what we were doing. To start things off, I ordered some great big Fathead® wall stickers to put up in my office and around the common office areas to let folks know it's okay to have some fun with how you decorate your work space.

Within a few days, I came to work and there were movie posters on the ceiling in the Customer Service area. One customer service rep added holiday lights to their cube and another hung up Area 52 conspiracy signs. Next thing you know, I go into the bathroom and there is a pee color chart letting you know if you are dehydrated or not. A few days later, someone added a smiley face to the bathroom mirror with a note saying "Smile, you're beautiful." There was also a new basket on the counter with a "help yourself" sign. The basket included everything from Q-tips and shaving razors to breath mints and cologne. The "don't pee here" stickers on the floor next to the urinals that eventually showed up were quite cute. Clearly there is more to including fun than just spicing up the office and one's work area, but that was the starting point. We also needed to really understand why having fun is important. To connect fun and productivity.

No, this wasn't from Halloween

A dress up day

Adding to Bonnie's Elvis collection

Just another dress up day

WHY SHOULD WE HAVE FUN AT WORK?

"Fun is one of the most important—
and underrated—ingredients in any successful venture.
If you're not having fun, then it's probably time to
call it quits and try something else."
—Richard Branson

If we include fun in what we do, work will be more enjoyable, period. It feels good to create it and feels good to participate in it. Research clearly shows happier employees are more productive. With a growing company that has endless to-do lists and meetings along with customers needing attention, vendors wanting time, training, and an overall super busy environment, the how becomes easier once you get the why.

Our questions and answers gave us a good idea where we needed to improve and some ideas on what and how to go about doing it. Understanding the why was really the ongoing spark to keep the fun going. Day by day and week by week, this guiding principle got to high speed at RealTruck.

We created a lot of events, from dress-up days and themed potlucks to doing rock star welcomes for new employees and visiting partners. A personal favorite of mine was a William Shatner birthday party, where we celebrated his birthday with some cake and someone made signs we could hold over our faces for a picture. The picture looked like a bunch of William Shatners having a good time. To top it off, we sent him a birthday card wishing him a wonderful day.

Our marketing and brand teams joined in and started adding some fun to our website, our products we offered, customer emails, marketing materials, product videos, and the meeting the team and customer thank you posters we created. The website got an overhaul as well to add some fun, from how pages were written to some of the banners and imagery. Our personalized and auto-

Justin and Josh rapping a birthday video

Shawn in a So Hot So Fresh video

Fun sock day

Mystery Machine

Football day

Including fun at a summer picnic

mated emails got a fun makeover. Some of the customer serendipity like our T-shirts and fuzzy dice also showed this.

To support this principle, marketing began making guiding principle videos in a fun manner that offered information on how to and how not to practice these principles. In addition, how RealTruck works, hiring videos, holiday videos, and even spontaneous "what employees think of RealTruck" videos began rolling out. The brands and video teams started including some fun in the product fast fact and installation videos.

Other departments also jumped in and somehow, for some of the holidays, each department would shoot a quick video—themed for that holiday, such as the 4th of July—and get together and do a music parody video. Then the company would vote on which one was the best.

The employee parties were events everyone looked forward to as they included everything from superheroes to gangster themes. We had them at hotels, theme parks, movie theaters, and more. We created bring your kid to work days and even bring your job to school days, where we went out to schools and had fun sharing with kids what we did at RealTruck. For some of these events, we dressed up in *Star Wars* outfits and other get-ups to add some fun. We were known for inviting our neighbors around the offices to attend some of our shorter one-hour parties we had for whatever was going on that week, from quick St. Patrick's day celebrations to regular employee birthday parties. It felt great to share the fun with others.

Company wide activities were also being created, such as the RealTruck Olympics, in which everyone participated. This was an event that included paper airplane contests, chair spins, and more.

Every department became involved and developed their own ways to include fun in what they were doing. Meetings would start or end with something fun, like a quick contest, game, or team-building exercise.

Other fun activities were confined to specific departments. For instance, marketing developed their own unique front page banners and promotions for the company.

Library Day at RealTruck

Happy birthday, William Shatner

My birthday desk

Paper airplane contest

RealTruck Olympics

Development created cool "Why work at RealTruck" videos. They also started a tech-tips and app-tips email that was shared with new employees. It included shortcuts, activities, and cool apps that could help the employee personally or professionally.

Each department was budgeted with funds specifically for culture building, from team lunches to training, gifts, or whatever else they wanted to use it for.

OMG, the awesome get togethers! There was our flapper-style mystery murder party as well as the many "play" casino nights. Mega fun. The Jamestown High Five Hallway and vendor welcomes were a thing of legend. Can't forget the RT talent show or the inflatable bouncy houses! And yes, the finger painting for new employees was also an interesting experience that ended with them doing painted handprints on the office walls.

As mentioned in a previous chapter, a job posting might include something like: asbestos-free environment, bottomless coffee, and the ability to wear a superhero cape without anyone thinking twice. Our help wanted ads, interviews, basic training, and customer service training all reflected this principle.

Fun also made its way to our partners with videos as well. At the Specialty Equipment Market Association (SEMA) show, the brand and market teams created "Include fun at SEMA" videos that were hilarious for partners and customers alike. Rather than the typical, check out this product video, there were examples of our fun, deliver more, and improve kind of culture. We did interviews with partners, celebs, and so forth with a very humorous tone. We also began filming partner arrivals and capturing the rock star welcomes so partners could share their experience visiting RealTruck with the folks back home.

We created annual awards for partners that best practiced our guiding principles, which included trophies and a grand awards ceremony. It was cool visiting vendor offices to see that our award was one of their most prized awards.

Some may be thinking, I'm not a fun person, what do I do? My answer is, participate in it. Support it. Like all guiding principles, some are easier to practice than others for each person personally. For this one, at a minimum, we can participate. Participation is key to feeling connected, especially at work. This chapter will end with some pictures attempting to capture where and how we have fun. This quote from Michael Jordan pretty much sums up this idea.

"Just play. Have fun.
Enjoy the game."
—*Michael Jordan*

...

Web Developer wanted posting

Meet the Team postcard with Tami

We Are Hiring videos

Include Fun poster

Happy Something Day

Web site banner

9
BE HUMBLE

"Talent is God given. Be humble.
Fame is man-given. Be grateful.
Conceit is self-given. Be careful."
—John Wooden

We must be respectful of everyone and treat everyone just like we would want to be treated if we were in their position. There can't be anything that needs to be done that is beneath me. Our successes are important, but we must not let that go to our head. We should not praise ourselves, but rather let our customers, partners and coworkers do it for us. An ethic of giving back and forward is highly valued. Being grateful for what we have, not taking anything for granted, being of service, helping others reach their fullest potential, setting up others for future success and making the future better is the spirit of being humble. When praised, we should give thanks and pass on credit. When we fall short, we should accept responsibility by being willing to correct and learn from it.

6. Be Humble

WHAT DOES BEING HUMBLE REALLY MEAN?

Be Humble is probably the hardest principle to practice and also the most rewarding. It's important we don't ever toot our own horn but rather let our customers, partners, and others do it for us. The essence of this principle is that we should praise others, pass on credit for success, and accept responsibility for failure. We should always be trying to make something better or easier for the next person. There shouldn't be any job or task below you. There might be something better for me to do, but there shouldn't be something below me to do. We need to keep our minds on being grateful for what we have.

Following the tradition of the other guiding principles, to get this going in our culture we started asking questions. Most of the be humble questions were personal in nature, designed to help us see where we are at. Our answers began to move us toward taking more actions that supported trying to practice humility.

BE HUMBLE QUESTIONS

- When is the last time I passed on credit to someone else or the team for something we did?
- How many times a day do I compliment someone?
- When is the last time I happily did something, helped someone, or volunteered to help that wasn't my job?
- When is the last time I complimented a coworker?
- When is the last time I complimented my boss or reports?
- What are 3 things I can do in my job to make it easier or better for the next person?
- How much time do I spend each week volunteering to help others?
- What are 3 things I can do anonymously that involve random acts of kindness at home, at work or around the community?
- What are 3 things RealTruck can do to give back to employees, partners or the community?
- What are 3 things I can do to give back to my coworkers?
- When and what was the last genuine compliment I gave someone?
- When was the last time I genuinely thanked and conveyed real appreciation to a customer, coworker or partner?
- What are 3 things I appreciate about my coworkers?
- What are 3 things I appreciate about our customers?
- What are 3 things I appreciate about our business partners?
- Take 15 minutes and write a gratitude list. Share it with 3 people.

Clearly the answers that came back from questions like these varied from person to person. But it got us all thinking about this principle, where we were at, and some ideas on practicing it better. We really wanted to create random acts of kindness, not random acts of content. Slowly you could see it making its way into our culture.

For me, when it came to showing appreciation to employees, I always felt it in my heart but with an ever-growing staff, I found it hard to stay up to speed with sharing and showing this appreciation for each of them. With folks I worked directly with, it was easier. But with everyone, much more difficult. Sure, a company-wide email or video expressing gratitude or a company-wide gift was nice, and something I did, but it really wasn't very personalized and difficult to really feel the real appreciation I felt. RealTruck would not be what it is and where it is without the help of lots and lots of great folks along the way.

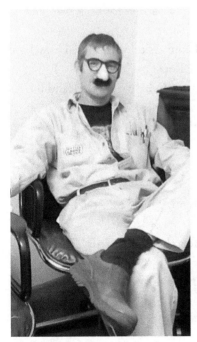

Getting ready to do a What's Up at RT video

Jeff and Justin getting ready to give some buttons

THE SECRET WEAPON

Often employees do not feel appreciated enough at work. We needed to change this and the real game changer was upon us. It started with managers, at the weekly meeting, shouting out or praising, one person in their department and one person from outside of their department for practicing one of the guiding principles.

These shout outs were included in my weekly "What's up at RT" videos that were shared with everyone in the company. The shout outs included three things. 1. Who. 2. What they did. 3. What guiding principle it was an example of. Here are some examples of these shout outs.

- Shout out to Jenny for delivering more to a customer by staying on the phone with the customer for 90 minutes, 40 minutes past her shift ending, to assist a customer with getting the right item for their vehicle in time for a trip.
- Shout out to Tami for sending flowers to a partner for their birthday. A great example of delivering more.
- Shout out to Lucy for having a candid conversion with me on how I can be a better employee. Transparency Rocks.
- Shout out to Josh for taking the extra time to help us understand the new product editor and creating a training video for it.
- Would like to give mad props to Jenny for starting to learn yoga and passing what she is learning on to me. Great example of improve.
- Shout out to Nate and Mary for re-organizing and cleaning the break room.
- Take risks shout out to Shawn for changing how we do the brand manager meetings.
- Shout out to Lindsey for making the new thank you cards. This is a great example of take risks.
- Would like to thank Anna and the team for surprising me on my birthday. Way to include fun.
- Shout out to Johnny for directing the Michael Jackson "Thriller" parody video.
- Thank you big time to Bonnie in accounting for helping with customer

Awards given to our partners

Vendor awards badges

RT friends and family at the Fargo marathon

service postcards, way to be humble.

Shout out to Chad for taking it on the chin for the rest of us when we incorrectly loaded a partner's data. The partner was very upset. Chad took the blame, asked how we could make it right. Got a few of us to stay late and fix the issue. Thanks for being humble.

Employees loved being mentioned in these videos. You could just see it. What about the folks that didn't get shouted out? Well, two things. First, over time a lot of folks from around the company did get praised for practicing a principle in the video. Second, the marketing team initially came out with bracelets that had a guiding principle on them. These were put in baskets around the company. Folks were asked to give them out to someone whenever they saw them do something that was a great example of practicing a particular guiding principle. Over time, we would have pins, buttons, and more with guiding principles on them to be used for this.

HUMILITY IN ACTION

What began to happen was amazing. Employees started catching each other doing things right and complimenting them for it. Sometimes they would even take pictures of receiving the guiding principle bracelet and share it on our private Facebook page that all employees could see. Eventually this became common practice all around the company. Our private Facebook page evolved into an endless daily stream of employees praising other employees and sometimes partners when they demonstrated our guiding principles in action.

It was amazing to see. For me personally, it was really an extension of my appreciation for each of them, mentioned earlier, that I wasn't able to give them in a personalized manner. The receiver felt appreciation and the giver felt good too. When you have an entire company of people all catching each other doing things right, it really propels growth and innovation, and you have happy and appreciated employees. It really connected the dots on what a particular guiding principle was and a real life example of practicing it.

A customer dressed up his truck to help a cause

Helping at the Ronald McDonald House

I've seen someone in accounting who showed up to work before maintenance arrived in order to shovel the snow on the sidewalk. I have seen an IT person pick up the phone and take a call during the busy season to help out. Amazing stuff.

Our customer service manager started cutting out all the customer emails praising us and putting them on a wall for everyone to see. I thought, in all my time of buying things online since 1998, very rarely have I emailed the company to tell them how impressed I was or how well they took care of me. Yet our walls were out of room from all the praise we received from our customers. We were humbled repeatedly.

I've watched a customer service rep shout out another customer service rep for taking the longest call in RT history. I watched accounting give our bean counter awards to folks in every department for saving us money or making something more efficient. The spirit of humility was growing at RealTruck. It was enhancing our business, but even better, it was enhancing people's lives. To see and feel appreciation is huge.

We created guiding principle awards for our partners for being great examples of our principles. We also did everything from partner appreciation phone calls to gifts and more. Things like these kept evolving over time. It was fairly common for flowers or candy or RT fuzzy dice to be going to customers, partners, and employees on a daily basis.

There were many things we did to support being humble in the company. Encouraging people to step up and serve others and take a service-first approach was always something wonderful to be part of. Donating time to charities like the food pantry or helping out the Ronald McDonald House were good examples too. With service leadership becoming more and more visible within our culture, you never knew from week to week what we might be helping out with. This service ethic resonated well with everyone.

We also wanted to serve our community better. We began volunteering for Meals on Wheels for the elderly in the community. In addition, we set up a charity of the quarter; we raised donations from the employees and the company

Raising the bar on birthdays

Jenn receiving a humble gift

FedEx having a party in our parking lot

would match the contribution. We made this process exciting by announcing these activities to the company and marketing them, and then others would go above and beyond. They produced fun videos, announcing what we were doing and how we needed help or volunteers, that were distributed to everyone in the company.

We started teaming up with UPS and United Way to help with food raising charity work. Employees got a real thrill and feeling of gratitude every time we reached out to the community to be of service.

I'd like to think some of our customers and most of our partners understood we really appreciated what they did for us. We tried to show them with our attitude and actions. Some of them really floored us with their kind words and reciprocal actions. UPS featured us in a national advertising campaign. What an honor. Some of our partners gave us awards like customer of the year and best e-commerce company. Our customers gave us praise by their letters and by recommending us to their friends. The percentage of returning customers continued to increase. And with an e-commerce company, that is a good predictor of future success.

This principle helped us keep our minds focused on being grateful and our actions centered around being of service. I get a great deal of praise for founding and leading RealTruck. Often, when a company has success, the leader is

A partner made us this sign

Be Humble poster

given the credit as if they did it by themselves. I'm not sure about those other companies, but for RealTruck, the real praise and credit goes to the people of RealTruck. If it was just me, RealTruck would still be in the basement or not exist. The reality is that it is not me who made RealTruck a success. It was the staff. The people of RealTruck were empowered to practice the values they personally had at work. This was the magic. It was also like the other guiding principles, a work in progress.

There is nothing more rewarding than helping others achieve and do better things than they thought they could. Thank you to the folks of RealTruck for helping me create and be a part of something way better than I thought I could or would.

> **"***Humility is the true key to success.***
> ***Successful people lose their way at times.***
> ***They often embrace and overindulge from the fruits of success.***
> ***Humility halts this arrogance and self-indulging trap.***
> ***Humble people share the credit and wealth,***
> ***remaining focused and hungry to continue the journey of success.***"**
> **—Rick Pitino**

...

CHAPTER 9

10
THE RESULTS

"Your personal core values define who you are,
and a company's core values ultimately define
the company's character and brand.
For individuals, character is destiny.
For organizations, culture is destiny."
—Tony Hsieh

nce our guiding principles were in place and there was buy-in from employees, sales numbers grew almost overnight. Our customers kept coming back and bringing their friends. Partners were lining up wanting to do business with us. Finding new employees became easier. We were not perfect, but we were growing emotionally as a company. Keeping existing employees became easier. The real reward was we were making people's lives better.

We weren't doing over-the-top grand things like inventing the next best gadget or creating the next life changing solution. We were improving the lives of the people around us, our staff, customers, and partners in little ways. Creating positive experiences and memories on a daily basis. We were not perfect; we were an ongoing, never-ending work in progress moving in the right direction.

Our employee, customer, and partner feedback clearly showed we were getting better and becoming a great business that just happened to sell pickup accessories online. We were known for pickup accessories, but better yet, we were known for how we made people feel. As a entrepreneur, knowing my business is impacting people's lives in a positive way is fulfillment on steroids.

A SHAVED HEAD

I promised to shave my head bald and donate the hair to charity if we made it to the $10 million dollars in sales mark. Guess who ended up bald? I did the same thing when we hit $25 million. And in RealTruck fashion, it was videoed and shared out. Berma, North Dakota's only female barber, even joined in on the fun and helped make sure the hair was cut in a manner that it could be used by the charity. It was hard to top as our sales grew year after year.

The benefits were clear from within and outside of our company. The improved results were everywhere. Revenue increased, return rates decreased, margin increased, expense decreased, positive rating increased, and of course, profit increased.

We created a profit-sharing plan for employees that was based on tenure, responsibility, and how well they practiced the guiding principles that was paid out quarterly. We had to hit our revenue and our profit goals. 50% of the profit was paid out to employees. We hit or blew away our goals every quarter.

Buzzing my hair when we hit our goals

First award for innovation in 2006

THE AWARDS

We received awards from partners, the community, and industries including:

- BizRate Platinum Circle of Excellence (Multiple years)
- North Dakota Young People's Top 3 Best Places to Work (Multiple years)
- Prairie Business Magazine's Top 3 Best Places to Work (Multiple years)
- Internet Retailers Top 300 Mobile
- Internet Retailers Top 500
- Internet Retailers 14th fastest growing
- Internet Retailers 8th fastest growing mobile
- IRCE Mobile Commerce Excellence Awards Finalist. RealTruck was alongside Lancôme, who won along with eBay and Wayfair
- Customer of the Year awards from numerous manufacturers and wholesalers
- Inc 5000 list. Fastest-growing in North Dakota one year
- Featured in UPS national ads
- Growing Jamestown Award
- Innovation Award from the Information Technology Council of North Dakota

Often folks ask, how did you pay for all this culture building stuff? First, we bet if we could get the culture right, everything else would work out and improve. Second, some of our marketing budget was used for culture activities. As more and more customers were referring us to their friends, we didn't have to spend as much money onboarding new customers. Since our partners really liked doing business with us, they gave us better deals. Since the entire company was actively enhancing and practicing our guiding principles, we didn't have to spend as much finding new customers, partners, or employees. It's the best investment we ever made.

...

CHAPTER 10

Mobile Top 500

Lucky to be featured in a UPS national ad

NDYP Award

Young Peoples' Award

"Great leaders help their people see how they can directly impact the company's objectives and their own personal goals."
—Chip Conley

11
E-COMMERCE CONCEPTS

"I don't think that you can invent on behalf of customers unless you're willing to think long-term, because a lot of invention doesn't work. If you're going to invent, it means you're going to experiment, and if you're going to experiment, you're going to fail, and if you're going to fail, you have to think long term."
—Jeff Bezos

This is a quick chapter on some e-commerce concepts I believe in. They were developed over time through sometimes easy and sometimes hard lessons, along with some trial and error. This is not an in-depth chapter on every aspect of e-commerce, rather an overview passing on some ideas and attitudes that helped RealTruck and other ventures with which I have been involved.

Better to be great at a few things, rather than good at many. This applies to everything from marketing to search engine optimization. This is not going to be a chapter on "how-to" e-commerce, rather the concepts and best practices that have helped the various businesses I have been involved with. My experience has been to keep this general idea, of being great at a few things, in the forefront of your mind in everything you do with respect to an e-commerce business.

- Better to do a few things really great than a bunch of mediocre things for your customers
- Better to rank in the top 5 for a few keywords than in the top 50 for a bunch of keywords
- Better to be great at one social media channel than mediocre on

> 50 of them
- Better to be an expert in one product category or service then mediocre in a bunch
- Better to master one digital advertising method than be average in all of them
- Better to sell a few products well than 1,000 products poorly
- Better to market a few things really well than a bunch of things poorly

In the U.S., e-commerce represents about 13%[11] of what is sold and is growing at 15+%[12] a year. It will be 50% in short order. It is not too late to get started. Embrace the idea that you want to get your brand or products to people whenever and however they want them.

If you are running an e-commerce company and more than 20% of your sales are over the phone, you are not doing a very good job making it easy for customers to purchase products online. If you were, the amount of phone sales would be minimal.

If you are a company that has 0% of your business via e-commerce, you better get going. If you are holding off because you are protecting your dealers, distributors, or some other old business philosophy, realize this is the future. Grow or die.

Be useful to your customer base in everything you do. Help them do whatever they do better. Gander Mountain[13] went broke because all they did was sell stuff. They didn't help anyone hunt, fish, camp, or sport better. They just sold stuff and tried to be all things to all people. They tried to be cheapest, they tried to have the best customer service, they tried to sell just about anything. Their website had shallow content and their marketing was all about buy, buy, buy. Clearly it didn't work.

---

11   Source: Digital Commerce 360 and Internet Retailer analysis of U.S. Commerce Department figures
12   Source: U.S. Commerce Department
13   *Chicago Tribune,* May 1 2017

Know why your company exists; this is important for marketing. It needs to match up. Most great e-commerce companies have a mission beyond just selling something.

Manage your expectations very well and consistently deliver on them. If you have a best price or low price guarantee policy that links to an 8-page legal document that contains lots of red and italicized text, you are over-promising and will be under-delivering. That is a good bad example of not properly managing expectations. You will disappoint more people than you will gain from advertising something like that. If you are marketing hassle-free returns, ask yourself, what return is ever hassle free? It's a pain in the ass, even when it goes smoothly. This is another example of over-promise and under-deliver. If you market something, make sure the customer's experience matches it. Advertising 10% off and then having exclusions for it is another example.

Be an expert in your space digitally. Digital marketing is growing so fast. This is not something you can hire out 100% on a full-time basis. Yes, you need partners, but pick them well. Master one area digitally, then move to the next space as you can support it. This goes back to, be great at a few things rather than average at many.

If you can master a digital marketing area before your competitors, it can keep you ahead for years. The advantage of mastering Facebook natural or paid ads ahead of your competitors, exponentially benefits you down the road because you then have time to master the next great digital marketing area.

Same thing applies to social media marketing. There are 200+ social media sites out there. Pick the ones you are going to master wisely. Master one, then move to the next rather than doing an average job on all of them. Yes, you want to get all the profiles you think you might use, but focus on one and get it rocking.

Since analytics makes tracking everything easy, most of your paid advertisements should be a calculation based on return on ad spend. Rather than a fixed advertising budget, figure out your ROI on it, and target that rather than having "fixed" ad budgets.

Load a few products and get them selling. Figure out why they are selling before you spend the time loading 10,000 items that don't sell.

Vet third-party providers well. Since I started and even now, there are lots of people trying to make money on people and brands that want to sell online or grow their current e-commerce. Pick them wisely; they can cost you a lot of money and time if you don't. Companies tend to over-promise and under-deliver, and it's often hard to tell where one third-party service ends and another begins.

Technology companies tend to try to further penetrate their existing customers by offering more technologies and services, which doesn't mean they are good at it. It's hard for a digital marketing company to be an expert in Google and Bing pay per click, then be masters in Google, YouTube and Facebook display ads, and be awesome at YouTube in stream ads, and be masters at Facebook, Google and YouTube retargeting, and be masters at Google shopping and Facebook shopper. They are most likely masters in one area and average in the others.

Another example of this is that it could be easy to get hooked up with a company that has a product recommendation engine, has software to offer customers, and product recommendations that they would be most likely to buy. This digital intelligence costs X amount a month, and here are the stats to show how it increases sales. They also have a reporting interface. Realize, it is their interface providing the data and the reports that make it look like they are doing their job, which they may or may not be. Make sure the stats and the recommendations make sense based on what you already know. Check it across the entire site. Otherwise you will be paying thousands of dollars for the same results you were getting by having your staff associate the recommendations.

Trust but verify. When it comes to web developers and technology companies, it's easy to believe they are smarter than you and therefore know what they are doing. This is often true; however, just like a writer needs a proofreader and editor, website development and related technologies need to be highly vetted on all devices and platforms. Test it more than once and test it under lots of conditions. Just because someone says it works doesn't mean it does.

Test, test, test. Verify, verify, verify. This applies to all development and all integrations.

For development, it's easy to have 15 projects 90% done. That's like having a ticket to the moon you can't use. It feels good, but it's worthless. It's worthless to you, the customer, and the developer. Step back, ask what is the minimum that can be published, and get that published. Often we want everything absolutely perfect, but remember we are building an always-improving experience. Publish smaller pieces of the whole faster.

Be transparent. Customers expect that. Shipping times, shipping costs, product reviews, warranty information, and so forth. If you know it, put it out there in an organized manner. Before I sold RealTruck, I was debating on putting warranty rates and reasons online with products, along with ship damage rates. Why? Because just like customer reviews, it helps the better products rise to the top and helps manufacturers improve their products, particularly when they see how they stack up against other brands.

Use your website. Your staff should be using your website to place orders; they will be one of your best resources for finding bugs and coming up with solutions for making the customer experience faster and better. They can't do that if they are placing customer orders on some back-end system. Customers may occasionally call, text, or email an issue to you, but most customers will just move on and you won't even know you have an issue.

Make decisions. Nothing will hurt you more if you or your staff are slow or scared to make decisions to move forward. You will make bad ones and good ones. Learn as you go. But no decision is a decision, and that is the surest thing to kill your progress. Remember, you can always change it as you go based on new experience and information.

What would an e-commerce team look like? If you have the funds for an entire team, here is what mine would look like. If you are a traditional company, I would NOT put the e-commerce team under your current VP of Marketing. That's the fastest way to fail. If they knew what they were doing, you would already be spending 50% or more of your ad budget on the digital space and your website would be kicking ass. There is nothing traditional about e-commerce and with mobile being 50+% of the traffic, that is even more clear.

E-commerce Leader
- Digital Marketing Manager
  - » DM Specialist PPC
  - » DM Specialist Catalog (Product Ads)
  - » DM Specialist Display
  - » DM Specialist Retargeting
  - » DM Specialist Social Ads
  - » DM Interns (as many as you can)
- User Experience Manager
  - » Web Project Manager
    - ○ Front End Developer
    - ○ Back End Developer
  - » Graphic Artist
  - » Content Manager
    - ○ Email Marketing Specialist
    - ○ Search Engine Optimization
      - * Web Content Specialist
    - ○ Social Media Manager
      - * Social Media Coordinator
      - * Social Media Interns
- Web Content Manager
  - » Analytics Specialist
  - » E-commerce Manager
    - ○ Conversion Specialist

You may be thinking, that's nice, but we don't have that kind of money to spend on a team, what are the other options? One would be to start with an e-commerce leader. Someone who has worked with web developers, digital marketers, social marketers, search engine optimizers, user experience folks, and build from there. They will guide you.

Another option is to start learning it yourself. Start with the website and work from there. There are tons of platforms like Woocommerce and Shopify you can start with. There are also tons of free and paid resources on YouTube and Google for the area you want to learn about.

Lastly, you just have to start. Ideas are plentiful. Action is the magic. Chances are, everything you need to start has already been developed by someone and can be used or bought, fairly inexpensively. When we built the first shopping cart, it took a lot of time and money. Today they are way better and much cheaper. You have to start. Good luck and feel free to ping me if you need some guidance.

...

> "E-commerce marketing isn't just a shiny website and slick ads.
> It's ideas, attitudes and actions that benefit the customer,
> the staff, and the brand's business partners.
> A strategic way of life, that when properly executed,
> creates life-long customers, evangelical employees,
> helpful partners and yes, some profit to boot."
> —Scott Bintz

1. Deliver More

2. Transparency Rocks

3. Improve

4. Take Risks

5. Include Fun

6. Be Humble

12

#ASKANYTHING

"A lack of transparency results
in distrust and a deep sense of insecurity."
—Dalai Lama

O ver the years there have been lots of questions at work, socially, and when I've been out speaking. Some questions are easier to answer than others and some even have no adequate answer, at least from me.

When I was at RealTruck, we had an #AskAnything policy to support our Transparency Rocks guiding principle. Most questions came in via an anonymous posting system. Of course others would be asked directly at town hall and regular ol' planning meetings. The ones that came in via email or socially were often easier for me to answer, because I could think about them for a bit.

Part of trying to stay open-minded means that based on new experiences or information, I reserve the right to change my mind at any time. Over the years at workshops with Q and A, there have been lots of questions and answers. Some of these answers have evolved. I thought about ending the book with some of the more common Q and As that you might find helpful. They are organized for questions about business, RealTruck, personal, and miscellaneous.

Have a question? Hashtag: #PrinciplesToFortune #AskAnything and shoot it to one of these profiles. Thanks. :)

Facebook.com/principlestofortune/
Instagram.com/principlestofortune
Linkedin.com/in/scottbintz
Twitter.com/bintzness101

BUSINESS QUESTIONS

What do you consider the biggest barrier to starting a business?
> One's self. Doubting you can do it in the first place. Remove that and you are on your way.

What is the best investment you see today?
> Yourself. Investing in yourself, period.

What was life like running a multi-million dollar company?
> I grew into it, so it was just something normal. What changed was how people looked at me. How I saw myself was the same. It was very exciting and rewarding having a front row seat in a fast growing company. The greatest joy was watching people do and experience things they never thought they were capable of. The greatest challenge was letting other people help. You could be talking to our HR one minute about a new policy, then coaching a manager 10 minutes later on something, and then rushing out the door to catch a flight to meet with a business partner, and you recruited someone to drive you to the airport so you could return some calls which could be related to marketing or finance or just about anything else. It was exciting.

I have a business idea. How do you know when it's the right time to do it?

Folks often reach out and want my advice on a business idea or wonder what they should do. If you have an idea, just start rowing. Meaning, just start taking action and stop waiting for perfect conditions or feedback. The biggest battle is you starting and not being so concerned with what others think of your idea. #JustRow. Rarely will you find someone who likes your idea better than you do.

What's the best way to figure out what I'm passionate about?

If you don't know where you want to go or what you want to do, sometimes you just need to start paddling and your course will just come to you along the way. Do more of what you like and less of what you don't. You may even discover you need to turn the boat around, but that's because you started rowing in the first place.

What kept you going even when things weren't going right?

I never felt I was smarter or more skilled, so being persistent and determined was something I could control. But when the wheels fall off, having some great friends and business associates helped me evolve my perception on something enough to keep going. Life and business ebbs and flows. Having the right people in my life during the ebbs has always helped.

What are some good trade shows to attend for e-commerce?

I like the Internet Retailer show in Chicago in June every year. Etail and Shop.org also put on great trade shows for e-commerce.

How do you get ideas for a successful business?

Travel. I like to see how they do it in other parts of the U.S. and the world.

Why does it seem like a lot of traditional brick and mortar stores fail at e-commerce?

> Because they do. They try to fit an in-store customer experience into a website and now into a mobile experience. They are worlds apart. If you are not taking care of your customers, someone else will.

Why are there more and more e-commerce only companies?

> First, because brick and mortar stores aren't always meeting the needs of their customers. Second, many great e-commerce only companies have a mission greater than just making money, which customers appreciate.

Is it hard to start a business when you don't have a lot of money?

> It can be. How much you really need depends on the kind of business. A service business often requires way less money to start. If you want to start a car company, well then you are going to need to be able to raise some big-time money. Sometimes, it can be really low if you have the option to start a hobby business, when you are not working your regular gig, and build it up. If you have the passion, you can find a way. There are all sorts of ways to get money. Ideas are cheap, everyone has them. If all you have is an idea without action or contribution, it will be hard to find investors.

At what point do you walk away from your real job and pursue your real passion?

> When you are willing to fail. When your desire for fulfillment and purpose is greater than your desire for stability. Ask yourself if you are willing to work harder than you ever have. Are you willing to be all in?

When do I know it's the right time to pursue my passion?

Now. Ultimately pursuing a passion is like a relationship. We want to make it a "logical" one, but it's more of an emotional one we make. We attempt to justify it with logic when others ask about it.

What's the best way to get more customers for a business?

You will always get more business by servicing your existing customers more. Wow them. Keeping and enhancing current customers is cheaper than finding new ones, plus if you "wow" them, they keep coming back for years and share the news about your business for free.

Is it hard to get a business loan?

Yes, it can be. Bankers are not investors. They are bankers who make calculated loans based on your ability to repay and often with you putting up collateral. Ideas and new businesses usually don't have much for collateral assets. Once you are more established, have some profit and forward momentum, it's easier. It does pay to maximize your lines of credit during good times, so if you need some extra cash you have access to it. When times are tough or your business isn't doing the best financially, it becomes even harder to get a loan.

What do you mean, maximize your lines of credit in good times?

Yes, during good times, expand your lines of credit. That doesn't mean you are going to necessarily use it, just make sure you have it. For example with RealTruck, when we had grown to about 6 million we were planning for a bigger year, and the next year we only did about 6.2 million, so our cash flow got really tight. Normally our sales were like a spiral staircase and the one year it kinda flattened off. That was when gas prices went through the roof, truck sales went down, and RealTruck needed some money for some more web development that we really needed to do. Essentially, I had to sign off my house, sell a bunch of personal stuff, and beg my banker for a loan. I felt like I sold about everything to keep RealTruck afloat and that the banker was really putting me at a disadvantage for borrowing money at decent rates. I knew we would pull out of it, it was an adjustment, but you couldn't get a banker to believe it, so I kinda learned then this isn't ever going to happen again. I didn't want to be in the position where I had to get a loan, where I felt I had to sign my life away and allow a banker to tell me how to run my business. When you don't really need the money, banks want to loan it to you, and when you do really need to borrow money, when money is tight in business, banks generally don't want to loan it to you, especially if your business is going through a hard time.

REALTRUCK QUESTIONS

What was your inspiration for RealTruck?

Initially, an easier way to sell the access roll-up cover (bed cover). It evolved for RT to become an icon for how companies should teach customers, staff and partners. Really to make people's lives better. That was the longer and more impactful inspiration.

How did you come up with the idea of RealTruck?

A friend was going to school to be a web developer. That caused me to ask the question "could we put a website up and sell a bed cover on it?" That answer was, sure, why not, we can try, and so RealTruck began.

Do you still have anything to do with RealTruck?

No, not on a day-to-day basis. I still have a little equity in Truck Hero, which is the company that purchased RealTruck. Which isn't enough to have an opinion on why, what, or how they go about doing business.

Do you still work for Truck Hero and what is your relationship like with them now?

Currently I don't work for them. However, in business, you never know what might happen in the future. I think we have a good relationship. After I transitioned out of running RealTruck on a day-to-day basis, I took it easy for a little while. Then the CEO, Bill Reminder, asked me to come into Truck Hero and create a digital marketing and web development team and ultimately re-build the Truck Hero website. Once this was completed, I left to spend more time with family, write a book, and do some soul searching. The soul searching resulted in revitalizing my entrepreneurial spirit. From time to time, I wonder if they will need my leadership again or perhaps call and ask for my thoughts on something. They did suggest for me to be on an advisory board at one time, but I haven't heard anymore about it. Truck Hero merged RealTruck with another e-commerce company, Auto Customs. It's a huge organization now. My confidence is back, so my ego tells me I could run it better. However, the back to reality portion of my brain, tells me they probably wouldn't ask me, unless the e-commerce operations fell on really hard times. To my understanding, they are doing great sales wise.

Besides the culture, what else helped RealTruck grow?

What took RealTruck to the next level? We stopped paying attention to other businesses that sold truck accessories and started watching and learning from companies that were great at e-commerce in other industries. I wasn't following anybody in our industry, I was following Amazon, Cafepress, Musicians Friend, and other companies that were killing it on the Internet. We also focused on being really great at a few things and stopped trying to be all things to all people.

Do you regret selling RealTruck?

I wasn't as business savvy regarding transactions like I could have been. You only get to sell the same business once. And I wish that the folks who really helped turn RealTruck into a great company would be able to contribute as they once did. You change leadership and generally that means you also change those around the leader.

How did you come up with the RealTruck name?

So, I had this idea that if we took this commercial we made to sell this pickup cover, to set up a website and put that video online that maybe we could sell some online, this was in 1998. So, my buddy who was going to school for web development helped me and we had to get dial up and rent space on the server. He found this place in the back of an attorney's office and we went back there and there was one guy that had a bunch of computers, looked like a nerd, and he said, well, this is what we are going to do. Then he asked, "what are you going to name it?" And I said I don't know, I haven't gotten that far and he started rattling off names and one of them was RealTruck.

We got RealTruck up and in the first day we put it up, it sold a cover, and that's how it started. And three months later the site goes dead. Sam, my developer at the time, calls and no answer. He shoots up to the attorney's office and it's all cleared out. Everything was gone, however, he was an honest guy because he registered RealTruck in my name. I think he planned on being in business and it just didn't work out so he grabbed his server and went. You are kind of limited by your name only. A lot of times companies should have a bigger stop doing list than a start doing list. So, we discovered at one time 40% of our data was cars, we looked at the data and we only sold 3% for cars, so we just stopped selling car stuff. We just couldn't get past the name.

How did you get your funding right away?

I had a business at the time, Northwest Representation, Inc. I used the cash flow from that, which wasn't much. Realize, at the time, the main expense in starting was paying my friend for web development. I've borrowed money over the years, but it's not my favorite thing. The saying "ye who pays the fiddler, calls the tune" always echoes in my head. If you get over your head financially, someone else will be telling you how to run your business.

What was it like to see your strategic plan come to life?

Sometimes, when you hear a business story like mine, it seems like it was a well-executed business plan; this happened, then this happened and we floated off to wonderland and all is beautiful now. Business is like a pinball machine. First, you have to be willing to play and lose. Then you learn to work the flippers and better control the ball. At first you suck. Your value per quarter is pretty low. You keep working and learning to better control the flippers. From moment to moment you don't know what's going to happen or what's going to come your way. You learn to adjust as you go. You keep learning the game. Learn where the best places are to score points and where the worst places are to score points. Then when you feel like you have it mastered, you shoot the ball and realize the designer of the machine changed things up. New things are added, old things are moved around. Again you adjust and keep working the flippers. You work your tail off playing the game and get better at it as you go. Then one day, someone comes up and says "wow," you really have some points racked up on the pinball machine. Must be nice to be a natural at pinball.

How did you get your business going without any outside capital?

It was a hobby business I worked on after I got my day job work done. It also helped having some good connections and relationships. I paid for things I could afford as we went along. I knew the manufacturer of the pickup cover I was representing. Talked him into drop shipping the product once we sold it online. Then that became my trade reference to find other manufacturers to do that with. In the case with RealTruck, we drop shipped everything and we got our money within 3-4 days since customers paid by credit card and didn't have to pay the vendor for 30 days. We could grow as fast as we could sell.

How did you know free shipping would be a good idea?

I think sometimes you need to accept the brutal facts of the market situation. What I mean by that is that if you're going to sell e-commerce, you need to have free shipping, like it or not, that has become the norm. You just need to figure out how to do business with free shipping. Then focus on other things that you can do to differentiate yourself.

PERSONAL QUESTIONS

What do you want to do next?

A few things. Take a manufacturer that doesn't do e-commerce and e-commerce them up. Create a brand from scratch. Write a book and figure out how to massively market it.

Where did you go to college and what is your degree in?

Minot State University. BA Economics.

What in your mind is the best/smartest way to grow your wealth? I.e. stocks, buying land, etc.

I don't really know yet. I'm new to the concept of making money with money. At RealTruck everything we made went into growing the business. I'm finding real estate is where people with wealth seem to move towards. Property doesn't require a lot of people and seems to increase in value generally over time. Stocks are tricky; many "stock brokers" and "financial advisors" really sell financial products rather than truly understand the markets. But I am learning this space and it is challenging with a splash of fun and a pinch of concern.

In your life, do you feel like you have accomplished your goals that were set for you?

Yes and then some. With much amazement, I have surpassed my goals that I started with. I learned over the years that creating goals is important. Everything that is possible starts with the dream that it is possible. Visualize it first, then work toward it. I have experienced way more than I ever thought I would, especially from where my life started. As I've grown, I have set new goals to work towards.

What do you do now?

Spending more time with family. Also doing some travelling abroad with family. Some brand building with RHRSwag.com, an e-commerce company offering race car parts to dirt track racers, RHRBrew.com, an e-commerce company offering custom coffee for entrepreneurs. Involved with Red Headed Rebel®, which offers e-commerce consulting. Trying my hand at a little manufacturing. Doing property investment; e-commercing up self-storage facilities and some stock trading.

Did you ever start a business that failed?

Yes. My first business was selling greeting cards door to door. I've always been wired that way: have a hundred ideas and might take action on one. Started a business in college advising people that failed. Started a company called Cellular World selling cell phone accessories that failed. Shortly after, I started a company called Jimmy Quik Lawn Care and Painting, that failed. Within business, there are also many projects that fail. Failure happens. Just learn and move on.

Have you sold other businesses besides RealTruck?

Yes. I had another company, Northwest Representation, Inc. We represented manufacturers and set up dealers for them. I sold that company to a sales rep who worked for me. He bought me out over three years.

Before all the success, what was your biggest failure in business?

There were many failures along that way, not sure which would be the "biggest". I was able to quickly move on and look at those failures as learning lessons. There are a couple that come to mind. I was demoted at a job for running an "unauthorized" promotion, which led to receiving a national award. The demotion was hard on my ego at the time, but it pushed me in a new direction that was more rewarding. I started a business in college that failed. There were many as mentioned above.

When you were younger and dreamed of having millions of dollars, what did you want to do with it? And are you doing that?

I didn't really ever dream of "having a million dollars." I did however dream about being successful at something. Creating something good or making a difference. I also wanted to be able to take care of my mom and my family and not worry about money, which is the case now. Money wasn't much of a motivator for me per se; money was something needed to make something else happen. However, I did want to fly on a private jet and own a really nice Camaro. Score on both counts. It's nice to know you can go almost anywhere, anytime.

What makes you come up with your ideas to start your business?

I seem to always be thinking about business stuff. What's cool, what's interesting, how things work around business. Always have lots of ideas and sometimes take action on a few of them. Out of 100 ideas, I probably take action on one.

What's your dream car? Do you own it yet?

1969 Camaro. Yes. If I would have really thought that might have been possible, my dream car would have been a Porsche or Ferrari, but that didn't seem like a "realistic" dream car. I do have a Porsche.

How has becoming rich changed your life/lifestyle?

We don't have to worry about paying the bills month to month, which is a big relief. We have the option to do and see more like travel abroad easily or get first-class tickets to an event. If I want to learn something, I can drop what I'm doing and learn it. Also I get hit up quite a bit for money for one thing or another, which makes for some interesting stories and investment opportunities.

After the success you've had, what can you do to progress now as a businessman and person?

I keep learning. Reading books and watching videos from interesting people. I tend to do this in binges, but feel if I can get one thing out of a book or from someone sharing that I take forward, it's a good lesson.

What was your most significant setback / failure as an entrepreneur and did it benefit you in the long run?

I would say the biggest failure as an entrepreneur was that in the early days of RealTruck, I was an asshole from time to time. What I mean by that is I think I've always had a good heart. So when I would overreact I would feel terrible and try to make it right. But sometimes when it came to sticking to the mission and accomplishing something, instead of teaching and coaching people, I would be extremely rude and blunt. Things were happening so fast, I didn't even realize it. I didn't have the awareness and one day I walked into work and I was walking down the hall, approaching a young kid who worked for me, and he jumped out of the way and put his back against the wall. I said, relax. I thought, Oh my God, this kid is terribly intimidated by me. I had an open door policy. And it occurred to me, no one was using it anymore. When people make a mistake or don't think of something they should have done, they always feel bad about it. My words and actions would make them feel worse. I needed and desperately wanted to change this. For whatever reason, I'm really good at running the what-ifs through my head quickly. As a result, I often see little details quickly that are sometimes missed by others. I had to learn how to communicate these things in a constructive and helpful manner. That involved me being disciplined to slow down. Meaning, slow down how fast I walk, slow down my need to address something right now. I also learned I needed to ask more questions. Often in these situations, if I asked the right questions, their own answers would help them figure out for themselves what details were missed. I think just learning how to work with and communicate effectively with different kinds of people was huge.

It was also huge realizing that something easy for me to see doesn't necessarily make it obvious for someone else. Leadership would be my biggest failure and biggest recovery. I was going through some old RealTruck stuff the other day and it kind of made me sad; I was digging through boxes and some gifts people who worked at RealTruck and vendors and stuff had given me and how heartfelt they were, but it didn't start that way. In the early days people may have said Scott Bintz is a jerk. Today, I think they would say I'm insightful, have a good heart, and am a little weird.

MISC. QUESTIONS

What advice would you give to someone picking a career path?

> Pursue what you enjoy. What interests you. First, you will be better at it. And if you really like something, you have more motivation to figure out a way to make enough money to do it. Follow the money and you probably won't enjoy it.

How did you get 25 million video views on YouTube?

> Luck and timing. However, there are a few more keys to natural video marketing success. Consistency, along with the concept of creating useful and helpful videos for your customer base. Often, I see brands go and create a grand production. A video that requires too much time and way too much money. It's crazy expensive. They will post it up, get 500 views, and wonder why no one liked the new slick video as much as they did. Then create another grand production and publish it a few months later with the same result. The likelihood of a good return on investment is relatively low.
>
> Rather than try to create a viral video, my experience has been to create and post videos regularly with content that helps the customer do whatever they do better. Be useful, be helpful. These videos include genuine people, sharing their real thoughts and experiences, with less scripting and staging. They can be produced faster with minimal costs. I'm not suggesting "grand productions" should not be created from time to time, rather if you don't have the audience, which you will get from more useful, genuine videos, then it's a big waste of time and money considering no one sees them. Whereas lower cost, helpful videos have a great return on investment and ultimately help you become a trusted authority in your space.
>
> 1. Be Consistent: Regularly load up videos to YouTube or Facebook. I suggest eight videos a week.

2. Be Useful: Help your customers do whatever they do better. Create useful videos rather than just buy videos or boring product videos. How to and why videos. If it's a product video it should be quick and presented in a genuine "real" person and "real" experience context.

3. Be Genuine: Rather than doing a grand production once every six months, just do genuine videos with genuine people, talking in real terms with the general theme of being helpful.

4. Be Determined: Building an audience takes time. Be steadfast in producing "useful" and "helpful" content. Don't get so caught up in video perfection.

5. Make Sure To Optimize: The videos should be titled properly and include a good description. Make sure the captions are turned on or added to the video. Create playlists to organize your videos by content types.

6. Link It Up: Make sure your description includes a link to your website, as well as creating cards with additional links. (For Facebook, include a link and occasionally tag a product if applicable.)

7. Embed It: When applicable, embed the video into your website on the page or pages that are most relevant to that content.

8. Share It: Share it on the appropriate social media platforms. Share it with your employees and business partners. Include it in your emails. Share it more than once. Depending on the content in the video and the social platform, you may be able to share it out 4-12 times in a year.

What are some of the entrepreneurial skills someone just starting out or still in school can learn?

1. Learn to Learn: You need to learn to learn on your own. If you need to know something, dig in and learn it. Don't be scared to ask questions. That speeds up the learning curve. Especially if you are

asking someone who has been there, done that.

2. Persuasion: You can also call it selling or being business savvy. But you need to learn how to "sell" people on ideas, attitudes, and actions. And learn to re-package them and try again as it's a process sometimes rather than a single event, whether it's convincing someone they can do better than they thought they could, a huge business idea, or even the plan of action to execute a business idea. This is an art. And if you are an artist, you should be getting better at it over time.

3. People Skills: You can't be successful without people. The better you can really get to know people, the easier it is. What their interests are. Understand their personality. All types of people. Tolerance and understanding are the keys here. You need people to help you with what you are not good at, so you can focus on what you are good at.

4. Think Long-Term: RealTruck was just another overnight "20 year" success. Don't be so caught up in what am I getting right now; it will blind and cripple you for the future. If you are interning for a CEO of a company and getting paid $12/hour, don't just look at the $12/hour. You might be getting $500/hr from the experience.

5. Focus: Having a vision for something also requires a laser-like focus on the small things needed to make the bigger picture come to reality. Knowing which of those smaller tasks are is important. Especially when you are learning as you go. Always better to have one thing done than 80 almost done.

6. Perseverance: Most give up too easily when confronted with an obstacle. You must wire your mind to lean toward how can we do this, rather than why can't we. Most folks are quick to share why something won't work. You have to be the one to be determined enough to figure out a way through it or around it.

7. Get It Done Attitude: No one cares why you didn't do something.

Published is better than perfect. Your return on investment, whether it's money or time, comes from something completed. Having a million dollar, unsigned check in your pocket might feel good, but it's worthless. Something almost done, almost has value.

8. Follow Up: It's amazing, you know, in the early days of RealTruck when we were trying to get it started. We would have vendors fly in to try to tell us to sell their stuff and we would say "Yes, you bet we want to sell your stuff. Here is what we need." Seems like a huge percent of them wouldn't get us the stuff, they wouldn't get us the images, data files and all the things we needed to take on their products. I was always amazed by that. The thing that separated RealTruck and even me from a lot of other people was just simple follow up. Meaning, I learned early on in my life the most spiritual thing I can do, is do what I say I'm going to do, when I say when I'm going to do it, but if not, let someone know about the not, ahead of time. So if I can't make it I should tell you ahead of time, if I do say I'm going to do it I should do it, even if someone better comes along. I think the other thing is, no one's leadership style fits everybody; we all kinda develop differently.

9. Start: Learn to start. Often people want the idea, plan, or whatever to be perfect. Once everything aligns perfectly, then they will start. That's crazy. That's like saying I'll learn to dance after I learn to dance. Learn to start and adjust as you go. You will also learn to fail, which to overcome, requires starting again.

10. Repeat: Rinse and repeat. Learn what works and what doesn't work for you. Adjust as needed and repeat.

Thank you for taking the time to read the book. May your journey be rewarding. May you find the fortune you seek.

Smile and pass it on...

ABOUT SCOTT

Scott Bintz is on a mission to make people's lives better.

Currently involved in a number of business ventures from advising brands and e-commerce strategy consulting to board member duties and limited speaking engagements. Scott is considered an expert in e-commerce, business strategy, digital marketing & company work culture building.

Scott is described by others as a good kind of "crazy" serial entrepreneur. He is most known for founding RealTruck.com in a basement, which grew into a 100+ million dollar e-commerce super-store .

In the E-commerce sector he continues his involvement in Red Headed Rebel®, a marketing company that advises companies with e-commerce; RHRSwag.com, a racing parts website; and Red Headed Rebel Brew (RHRBrew.com), coffee for entrepreneurs, game-changers, rebels & rule breakers. He also created RH Rebel Storage, state-of-the-art self storage facilities.

In the racing arena, he picked up the nickname "Red Headed Rebel".

Scott grew up in Minot, ND, graduated alternative HS in 1989 and from Minot State University in 1993 with a BA in economics. He currently lives with his family in Jamestown, ND.

Scott would love to hear from you!

ScottBintz.com
Twitter.com/bintzness101
Linkedin.com/in/scottbintz
Facebook.com/scott.bintz
Instagram.com/scottbintz

PRINCIPLES
TO FORTUNE

VISIT:

PrinciplesToFortune.com

SIGN UP:

To Our Newsletter

SHARE:

Take a pic of the book, tag us and share it out

HASHTAG:

#PrinciplesToFortune

CONNECT WITH US SOCIALLY Ⓐ

Facebook.com/principlestofortune
Instagram.com/principlestofortune
Snapchat.com/add/scottbintz
Linkedin.com/in/scottbintz
Twitter.com/bintzness101

WANT AN AUTOGRAPHED COPY?

Order online at ScottBintz.com

SWAG
Up Your Office With
PRINCIPLES

1. Deliver More

2. Transparency Rocks

3. Improve

4. Take Risks

5. Include Fun

6. Be Humble

VISIT PrinciplesToFortune.com/Shop

CPSIA information can be obtained
at www.ICGtesting.com
Printed in the USA
BVHW052131301121
622870BV00002B/183